California DMV Exam Workbook

Your Ultimate Guide to First-Try Success with 450 Comprehensive Practice Questions and Detailed Breakdowns

Melvin Knowles

Chapter 1: Introduction to DMV Exam

1.1 Understanding the DMV Exam

Preparing for the DMV exam can seem daunting, but understanding exactly what the test covers and how it is structured can help you approach it with confidence. The DMV written exam is designed to assess your knowledge of critical driving laws, road rules, and safe driving practices. Passing this exam is required to get your driver's license.

The test covers information found in the California Driver Handbook, including:

Traffic Laws - You'll need to know state laws covering right-of-way, traffic lights, yielding, parking, and more. Laws prohibit actions like texting or calling while driving, and mandate practices like proper seat belt use.

Road Signs & Signals - Knowledge of regulatory, warning, and information signs is key. You must understand common signals, pavement markings, and lane markings as well.

Safe Driving - Questions test judgment required for safe driving. Examples include proper following distance, managing visibility and distractions, and recognizing impaired or aggressive drivers.

Vehicle Procedures - You'll need to know rules of the road when it comes to passing other cars, merging lanes, and maintaining speed. Procedures for purchasing insurance and what to do after an accident are also covered.

The exam is comprised of 46 questions with a passing score of 38 correct answers. There is no time limit, so work through each question carefully. Questions come in multiple-choice and true-false formats. The test is administered on a computer at your local DMV office. You can take the written exam even before obtaining your learner's permit.

It's essential to set aside dedicated study time and get lots of practice tests under your belt. Make flashcards for road signs, skim the handbook regularly, and take practice tests to identify weak areas. Focus particularly on any topics you consistently miss during practice.

As you study:

- Carefully review each DMV handbook section
- Memorize meanings of road signs, signals, and pavement markings
- Understand when to yield right-of-way
- Know speed limits for various zones and conditions

- Study proper following distance, parking laws, and safety procedures
- Brush up on requirements for license registration, titling, and insurance

It also helps to stay calm on exam day. Arrive early, on a full stomach, and well-rested. Read each question thoroughly and eliminate wrong answers. If stumped, flag the question and return to it at the end. With diligent preparation, you will gain the knowledge and confidence to pass this critical exam on the first attempt. Stay positive - you've got this!

1.2 Importance of Passing the DMV Exam

Obtaining your driver's license is a major milestone in life. While an exciting rite of passage, it comes with major responsibilities. The DMV written exam is critical for assessing your readiness to become a safe, law-abiding driver. Though passing seems daunting, the benefits of getting your license make the effort well worthwhile.
Once you pass, a new world of independence and opportunity opens up. The ability to legally drive unlocks more options for work, social activities, and life responsibilities. A driver's license serves as a valid state ID, useful for everything from writing checks to airplane travel. Having one also shows you are willing to take on the duties of driving, and opens up practical advantages like being able to rent vehicles.
Beyond gaining driving privileges, there are several key reasons why passing on the first try is so important:
You Save Time and Money - Failing means starting the process over from square one. You'll have to reschedule, retake the exam, and pay new fees, which varies by state but can be up to $70. This requires more time off work or school. The hassle and costs quickly add up if you fail multiple times.
It Shows You Are a Responsible Driver - Passing demonstrates your willingness and ability to learn the rules of the road. It requires studying the driver's handbook and practicing safe habits. This knowledge makes you better prepared for real on-road driving. Failing, however, signals a lack of driving competence or responsibility.
Your Insurance Rates Stay Low - Insurance providers view failing the exam as a red flag. This could impact your rates going forward. However, passing shows you take driving seriously and understand important laws and practices that reduce risk. Having your license for longer also helps lower insurance premiums over time.

You Build Confidence Behind the Wheel - Passing gives you confidence in your knowledge and skills. You can operate a vehicle assured that you know critical safety rules and techniques. Failed attempts lead to uncertainty and anxiety about driving illegally, while passing brings peace of mind.
A Clean Driving History Starts Now - Traffic offenses, accidents, and license suspensions down the road can really complicate things. But when you pass the first time, you start your driving career with a clean slate. Avoiding early mistakes means you can establish and maintain a strong lifelong driving history.
In summary, the DMV exam stands between you and an open highway of possibilities. Approach preparation proactively and diligently. Understand the reasons why passing matters - from freedom to driver's confidence. Remember that driving is a privilege and requires commitment. Rise to meet the standards expected of safe, knowledgeable drivers. Look forward to a lifetime of enjoying the open road once you successfully ace that test.

1.3 Common Myths about the DMV Exam

Getting your driver's license is an exciting milestone, but a lot of myths and rumors circulate about the process. Understanding what's true versus false can help you properly prepare for and pass the DMV exam on your first attempt. Let's separate DMV fact from fiction.
Myth: The DMV wants you to fail the exam to collect more retest fees.
Fact: The DMV does not have a vested interest in exam failures - their role is promoting public safety. Written and road tests assess if an applicant has mastered critical driving knowledge. While a failure does generate another fee, the DMV aims to administer fair, accurate assessments. Focus your energy on thorough test prep versus feeling the DMV is working against you.
Myth: The written exam asks crazy obscure questions to trip people up.
Fact: The DMV pulls exam questions directly from the driver's handbook. Therefore, studying the handbook ensures you learn the information needed to pass. While some questions may seem tricky, they assess legitimate driving knowledge. Read each question carefully and think through all the details. Avoid overcomplicating questions in your mind.
Myth: If you fail the written test, you have to wait months to retake it.
Fact: Most states only require waiting 1-2 weeks before you can retest after failing the written exam. Some even let you retest the

same day. Carefully review your state's specific retake policy so you know what to expect. Schedule your retest date as soon as the waiting window allows.
Myth: The exam asks mathematical questions and other tricky brain teasers.
Fact: The test focuses squarely on driving knowledge, not math skills or logic puzzles. Brush up on handbook sections like road signs, laws, and safety rules rather than memorizing equations. Some questions do require logical thinking, but no advanced math or puzzles appear.
Myth: Studying the handbook a few days before your test is sufficient.
Fact: Cramming is an ineffective strategy for the written exam. Give yourself weeks to thoroughly learn all the material covered in the handbook. Take practice tests to identify weak areas needing more focus. Developing long-term familiarity with the information is key. Don't underestimate the commitment required to pass on your first attempt.
Myth: You can pass just by relying on your common sense.
Fact: Common sense won't be enough to pass this exam. Even experienced drivers have gaps in knowledge that thorough studying can fill. Memorize precise speed limits, fine amounts, intersection right-of-ways, and other details. Don't assume the exam will align with your instincts - know the handbook inside and out.
Myth: The written test is extremely difficult and failing is very common.
Fact: While the exam does assess important driving competencies, passing is very achievable with diligent preparation. Many first-time applicants pass, especially those who study wisely, leverage practice tests, and commit to learning the material. Avoid psyching yourself out - have confidence in your readiness.
By learning the facts behind common DMV myths, you can better set yourself up for written exam success. Separate truth from fiction when it comes to advice and study strategies. The DMV wants to see every eligible, prepared applicant pass their tests. You now have the knowledge to approach the exam with clarity and confidence.

1.4 Overcoming Test Anxiety

It's normal to feel some stress about taking the DMV written exam. However, when nerves escalate into true test anxiety, it can negatively impact your ability to pass. Learning to keep anxiety under control is key to being relaxed, focused, and clear-headed on exam day. With the right mindset and prep strategies, you can overcome test stress and ace that exam.

First, realize that some pre-exam nerves are inevitable, but don't let them snowball. Anxiety thrives on irrational, negative thoughts. Counter fears of failure with positive self-talk. Remind yourself that you've studied diligently and are ready to show the DMV your driving competence. Visualize yourself passing and achieving your goal.
Next, ensure you're fully prepared in the weeks leading up to the exam. Cramming increases anxiety, while consistent, early studying boosts confidence. Make a study schedule and stick to it. Take practice tests to identify and improve on weak areas. Review the driver's handbook regularly, creating quizzes and flashcards if helpful. Knowing the material thoroughly will minimize stress.
On exam day, use calming techniques to self-soothe nervous thoughts. Deep breathing exercises help relax the body and mind. Visualize your happy place. Listen to soothing music on the drive over. Go for a brief walk to ease muscle tension. The more you can calm your mind, the more clearly you can think.
During the test, read each question slowly and carefully before answering. Rushing leads to careless mistakes fueled by anxiety. Think positive thoughts and affirm you know this material. If you start feeling overwhelmed, take a few deep breaths to refocus.
Flag any questions you're unsure of and revisit them at the end. This saves time versus getting stuck on a tough question now. Trust your instincts and don't second-guess answers excessively. Overthinking due to anxiety only leads to confusion.
Avoid fixating on how many questions you may be getting wrong or how much time is left. Stay focused in the present moment on answering each question to the best of your ability. Tune out nearby test takers so you don't start comparing yourself.
Remember that minor errors won't cause failure, only missing many questions will. Have faith in the weeks spent studying and practicing for this exam. If anxiety flares up, take another deep breath to clear your head before proceeding.
After the exam, do not dwell on questions you now worry you missed. That cycle of negative thinking only breeds more anxiety. Instead, reflect on what you can improve for next time and trust you did your best today.
With the right preparation and mindset, you can conquer test nerves. Have faith in your knowledge. Practice relaxation techniques. Visualize success. Stay focused on the present question, not past mistakes. You are ready for this - it's time to show the DMV what you know. Approach the exam feeling competent and in control.

1.5 Study Strategies for Success

Preparing for the DMV written driving exam requires more than just memorizing handbook material. You need an arsenal of targeted study strategies to master the knowledge and ace the test. Follow these techniques to make every minute of study time count on your journey to success.

Create a Study Schedule

Don't leave preparation to the last minute. Give yourself at least a month to study if you can. Map out a realistic weekly schedule detailing when and what you'll study. Block out mini-sessions several times a week versus cramming. Check off tasks as you go and adjust your plan if needed.

Take Practice Tests

Practice exams are your best tool for gauging readiness. Take timed tests regularly, increasing frequency as exam day nears. Grade yourself to reveal weak areas needing more focus. Mimic real test conditions by studying missed material after. Save some publishers' practice exams for closer to test day.

Focus on Handbook Sections

The handbook outlines everything assessed on the exam, so let it guide your studies. Highlight key laws, guidelines, and facts as you read. Jot down quick summaries of each section's must-know info. Then thoroughly review your notes and turn them into flashcards.

Learn Road Signs and Markings

Memorize what every road sign, pavement marking, and traffic signal means. Search online for DMV handbook visual study aids listing these. Test yourself by looking at a sign and recalling what it indicates. Group similar signs together when studying to connect meaning.

Study with Friends or Family

Turn study sessions into group activities. Quiz each other's knowledge of driving laws and handbook material. Teach topics you already excel in to reinforce the material. Having a study buddy keeps you accountable.

Explain Concepts Out Loud

Pretend you're teaching handbook concepts to an imaginary audience. Verbalizing the material reinforces retention and reveals holes in your knowledge. Mimic how you'd explain a rule or process during the actual exam when speaking out loud.

Use Memory Techniques

Connect information to vivid mental images and associations. For example, visualize a red STOP hand sign when learning right-of-way rules. Acronyms like SPEED (Signal, Pull over, Evaluate surroundings, Execute lane change, Drive away) help you remember steps. Chunk related rules together when memorizing versus viewing them in isolation.

Eliminate Distractions

Avoid studying anywhere with things that can break your focus. Put your phone on silent and stay off social media. Consider using focus apps that block sites during study sessions. Take breaks as needed, but don't let distractions sabotage productivity.

Get Plenty of Rest

Don't cram all night before test day. Log quality sleep to retain material and sharpen focus. Your mind consolidates information during rest, so late nights are counterproductive. Be sure to also eat a brain-powering meal before the exam.

In summary, approach your DMV studies strategically. Leverage varied techniques like practice tests, group studying, memory tricks, and eliminating distractions. Creating a smart study plan and sticking to it are keys to success. Be confident that diligent preparation will have you walking in ready to ace that test.

Chapter 2: Road Signs and Symbols

2.1 The Importance of Road Signs

The array of signs encountered on roads may seem endless, but each one serves a vital purpose. While driving, road signs provide critical information to help you navigate safely and legally. Understanding and obeying signs is essential for smooth traffic flow and accident prevention.

Road signs communicate laws, warnings, and guidance in a clear visual manner. Their standardized colors, shapes and symbols allow you to quickly grasp the message. Signs are designed to be universally understood at a glance despite language barriers. Just a few seconds spent reacting to a sign can make the difference in avoiding a crash.

Regulatory signs instruct driver behaviors and indicate legal obligations. For example, stopping at red octagons or yield signs is mandatory. Speed limit signs must be obeyed or you risk fines. Other regulatory signs dictate direction of travel, turning/passing restrictions, permitted vehicle types, and parking rules. Abiding by regulatory signs prevents chaos on the roads.

Warning signs alert you to possible hazards and dangers ahead, such as curves, lane changes, pedestrians, low clearance, merging traffic, and more. Caution signs prepare you to adjust speed and driving to adapt to risky conditions. Being able to identify and heed warning signs gives you time to react safely.

Guide signs provide key navigational information. They direct flow of traffic, point the way to specific destinations, and inform about services at upcoming exits. Following guide signs ensures you take the correct routes and don't get lost.

Understanding the meaning behind road signs allows you to drive defensively and avoid dangerous situations. For example, seeing a "Deer Crossing" sign prompts you to slow down and watch the road edges. An "Intersection Ahead" sign tells you to prepare to brake or stop. Seeing any sign gives you advance notice to make smart driving decisions.

In traffic, signs help organize the orderly flow of vehicles. Everyone obeying the same signs prevents collisions and minimizes congestion. Signs also reduce driver confusion and frustration. If every driver understands the messages signs convey, traffic progresses smoothly.

Road signs are your silent guides, giving you the information needed to drive safely from point A to point B. Make a habit of taking one last look for signs as you approach intersections or highway exits. Allow a brief glance to process the sign's meaning and respond accordingly. Never ignore or willfully disobey any posted sign, which constitutes a traffic violation. Mastering road signs equals mastering the rules of the road.

2.2 Common Road Signs and Their Meanings

Understanding road signs is a vital driving skill. While signs may seem confusing at first, learning what the most common ones mean will become second nature with time and practice. Memorize the following important signs to drive safely and pass your DMV exam.
Stop Sign - Red octagon with white letters. Come to a full and complete stop. Check for crossing traffic before proceeding. Right turn on red may be permissible after stopping.
Yield Sign - Red and white downward triangle. Slow down and be prepared to stop if necessary to yield right-of-way to oncoming traffic before proceeding.
Speed Limit Sign - Black and white rectangular sign displaying legal speed for that zone. Observe and obey the posted speed limit. Fines for speeding may apply.
No U-Turn Sign - Round sign with red slash through U-turn maneuver. U-turns are prohibited in areas with these signs.
Do Not Enter Sign - White square sign with red circle and slash. Vehicles are prohibited from entering the roadway/area marked with this sign.
One Way Sign - White rectangular sign with one black arrow. Traffic flows only in the direction indicated on one-way roads.
No Left/Right Turn Sign - Round white sign with red arrow showing turning direction prohibited. Find alternate route instead of turning in that direction.
Railroad Crossing Sign - Circular yellow sign with X and RR letters. Approach with caution and be prepared to stop for passing trains before crossing tracks.
School Zone Sign - Pentagonal yellow sign with black S. Indicates you are entering an area with increased pedestrian activity. Obey lower speed limit during posted school zone hours.
Pedestrian Crossing Sign - Yellow diamond sign with pedestrian graphic. Watch for people crossing road on foot and be prepared to stop.
Slippery When Wet Sign - Yellow diamond with black graphic of car skidding. Slow down and use extra caution during wet road conditions.

Deer Crossing Sign - Brown rectangular sign with deer profile. Watch for deer entering roadway, especially at dawn and dusk.
Merging Traffic Sign - Yellow diamond sign alerting drivers to merge safely with cars entering from a ramp. Match vehicle speeds for smooth merge.
Added Lane Sign - Black and white rectangular sign indicating that an extra lane is joining the highway. New traffic will be merging.
Wrong Way Sign - Shaped like a fish tail. Warns drivers going the wrong way on roads or ramps to stop and turn around.
By memorizing the common signs you'll regularly encounter, you can drive confidently and safely. Understanding signs only takes a split second but makes a world of difference in preventing accidents. Pay attention, focus on the signs, and heed their important messages.

2.3 Understanding Regulatory Signs

Regulatory signs play a crucial role in traffic control by informing drivers of required and prohibited actions. These black and white rectangular signs provide the legal parameters that govern roadways, serving an important law enforcement function. Learning to identify and obey regulatory signs is key to avoiding fines, accidents, and dangerous driving.
Speed Limit Signs
The most common regulatory signs display legal speed limits that are mandatory, not mere suggestions. Exceeding the posted limit constitutes speeding, although drivers may travel under the limit when conditions warrant extra caution. Standard speed limits apply unless otherwise posted, such as 25 mph in residential areas or 55 mph on highways. Be ready to reduce speed when entering school zones or construction areas.
No Turn Signs
These signs forbid turning in a specific direction, usually onto a particular roadway. No left turn and no right turn signs will display a red arrow pointing in the prohibited direction. They are posted at intersections where such turns are deemed unsafe or illegal. Always follow the sign’s instruction and plan an alternate route instead.
Do Not Enter and Wrong Way Signs
Drivers will see these regulatory signs if they attempt to enter a roadway against traffic flow, such as accidentally driving the wrong way onto a one-way street. Heed the signs immediately and safely correct your direction of travel to avoid collisions.
Passing Signs

Regulatory signs along rural highways either permit or prohibit passing slower vehicles. A "Do Not Pass" sign means you must not cross the center line. A "Pass With Care" sign indicates you may pass with caution in specified areas. Never pass multiple cars at once or when visibility is limited.
Parking and Stopping Signs
Signs will restrict parking, stopping, or standing along certain roadways. For example, "No Parking Any Time" signs prohibit parking in zones with high traffic volume. Signs also designate individual spaces reserved for persons with disabilities, loading zones, or police vehicles. "No Stopping" signs mean you cannot even briefly wait in your car along marked zones.
One Way Signs
These signs marking one-way streets only permit traffic flow in the indicated direction. Attempting to enter or drive the wrong way is illegal and highly dangerous due to oncoming vehicles. Obey one-way signs and be vigilant at intersections where wrong-way entry is possible.
By understanding the intent behind regulatory signs, you can become a safer, more informed driver. Look for signs approaching every intersection and anytime you attempt turns, passes, or parking. With a little practice, obeying important regulatory signs will come naturally.

2.4 Warning Signs and Their Implications

Warning signs play a vital role in roadway safety by alerting drivers to possible hazards ahead. These yellow diamond-shaped signs provide advance notice so you can adjust your driving to avoid danger. Understanding and heeding warning signs helps prevent accidents and injuries.
Curve Ahead Signs
These signs warn of a curve or turn in the roadway that may require reducing speed to maintain control through the bend. Slow down in advance of the sign to avoid braking suddenly in the curve, which could cause skidding. Keep a firm grip on the wheel and navigate the curve gradually.
Narrow Bridge Signs
Where bridges taper or tighten, these signs advise drivers to use caution. Narrow bridges can leave little margin for error. Adjust your vehicle position to keep centered in the lane and maintain slow, steady speed across the bridge. Be prepared to yield if crossing with oncoming traffic.
Low Clearance Signs

Tunnel height and overpass clearance is indicated so vehicles too tall avoid colliding with the structure. Ensure you clear the height noted on the sign with room to spare. Know the height of your vehicle and trailer or roof attachments.
Two-Way Traffic Signs
These signs on narrow roadways warn that there is oncoming traffic even without a dividing median. Drive to the far right, watch for approaching vehicles, and pass others with extreme care. Do not attempt to pass multiple cars at once.
Merging Traffic Signs
Where lanes combine, be prepared to allow vehicles to merge smoothly from ramps, lanes ending, etc. Adjust speed to open a gap for merging traffic. Avoid speeding up to close gaps or preventing merging.
Pedestrian Crossing Signs
Watch for people potentially crossing where these signs are posted near intersections, schools, parks, etc. Scan ahead and sides of the road for pedestrians. Reduce speed and prepare to stop completely to allow safe crossing.
Falling Rocks Signs
Where rockslides or debris may cross the road, use caution and reduce speed in case you need to brake suddenly or steer around obstructions. Do not stop in these zones because falling material can strike a stationary vehicle.
By taking warning signs seriously and adjusting driving accordingly, you gain extra reaction time to avoid hazards and collisions. Don't speed past them assuming conditions are safe. Slow down, be alert, and proceed with caution.

2.5 Guide, Service, and Recreation Signs

In addition to regulatory and warning road signs, there are also helpful guide signs providing navigation information to drivers. These green, brown, and blue signs identify routes, direct traffic, and indicate nearby services and points of interest. Understanding guide, service, and recreation signs assists with trip planning and staying oriented.

Guide Signs

These green signs are overhead or posted at intersections to identify numbered highways, direct routes to major cities/destinations, and notify distances. They guide drivers along the best path, identify upcoming exits, and help avoid getting lost.

Mile Marker Signs

Found along highways, these small green signs provide mileage count increments to inform drivers of their location and progress. Mile markers also help emergency services pinpoint accident locations.

Route Number Signs

Rectangular green signs help drivers follow numbered interstates and highways. Knowing your route number provides direction on multi-lane highways with split routes and multiple interchanges.

Destination Signs

These green signs indicate the direction vehicles must follow to reach major cities, facilities, or intersections along a route. They often denote two destinations with arrows pointing left or right.

Service Signs

Blue signs point the way to traveler necessities like gas, food, lodging and hospitals at upcoming exits. Logos represent the specific business types available. Plan pit stops and logistics using these service indicators.

Recreation Signs

Destinations like campgrounds, parks, and attractions are identified by brown signs. Follow them to recreational sites, many of which have suitable parking for vehicles with trailers.

Weigh Station Signs

Commercial trucks and vehicles over certain weight limits are required to pass through weigh stations when indicated by signs. Officers inspect vehicles and loads at these sites.

By paying attention to guide and service signs, you can stay oriented, identify amenities, and plan optimal routes. Let the signs point your way and allow ample time to safely exit or change lanes. With practice, navigating using highway signage becomes second nature. Just stay focused on signs rather than electronic maps or devices.

Mile Marker Signs

Chapter 3: Traffic Laws and Regulations

3.1 Basic Traffic Laws

Understanding fundamental traffic laws is essential for obtaining your driver's license and becoming a safe, responsible driver. While driving regulations vary slightly between states, core legal principles apply nationwide. Familiarize yourself with these key basic traffic laws.
Obey Posted Speed Limits
The maximum legal driving speeds are clearly signed along roadways. While conditions may warrant driving below the posted limit, exceeding speed limits is illegal. Fines typically increase the farther over the limit you drive. Some states add extra fines for excessive speeding.
Stop at Red Lights and Stop Signs
Failing to stop at intersections with red traffic lights and stop signs violates right-of-way laws. Come to a full and complete stop behind crosswalk lines or before intersections. Ensure crossing traffic has passed before proceeding. Exception: Right turns on red may be allowed after a full stop and yielding to pedestrians.
Yield Right-of-Way When Required
Cars must legally yield the right-of-way when other vehicles or pedestrians have the legal permission to proceed first. Common yielding includes allowing oncoming traffic to clear before turning left, letting merging vehicles into your lane, and stopping for crossing pedestrians.
Obey Lane Markings
Stay within lane markings and do not straddle multiple lanes. Follow arrows, symbols, and directions conveyed through road paint. Only change lanes when legal and after proper signaling. Crossing double yellow lines into oncoming traffic lanes is prohibited.
Signal All Turns and Lane Changes
Use turn signals to communicate every turn and lane change well in advance. Signal even when you do not see nearby vehicles, as other cars may enter your blind spots. Proper signaling gives other drivers time to react.
Wear Your Seat Belt
Seat belt use is required for drivers and all passengers in all seating positions, even backseats. Properly worn lap and shoulder belts greatly reduce injuries and deaths in crashes. Children must be properly restrained in child safety seats.
Obey Posted Signs and Signals

Adhere to all posted traffic signs, warning signs, lights, and road markings. These legally enforceable signals provide critical roadway information and instructions for safe, orderly traffic flow.
Provide Space for Emergency Vehicles
When an emergency vehicle approaches with sirens and lights activated, carefully move to the right side of the road and stop until it passes to provide a clear right-of-way. Following a fire truck too closely or blocking its path violates traffic laws.
Avoid Distracted Driving
It is illegal in most states to drive while texting, dialing phones, inputting navigation, or any other activity that diverts attention visually and mentally from the road. These dangerous distractions lead to accidents and huge fines.
Following basic traffic safety rules preserves public order, prevents accidents, and saves lives. Make lawful driving habits second nature.

3.2 Right-of-Way Rules

Understanding right-of-way is essential to navigating intersections safely and avoiding collisions. Right-of-way determines who has the legal right to proceed first when multiple cars or road users approach at the same time. Learn to properly yield right-of-way in all driving scenarios.
At Intersections
Traffic signs and signals legally assign right-of-way at intersections. A green light indicates you have the right-of-way to proceed straight or make any legal turns. Yield to oncoming cars before turning left on a green light. At stop signs, the first vehicle to arrive has the right-of-way. If simultaneous, defer to the car on the right.
At Unsignalized Intersections
When approaching an uncontrolled 4-way intersection, yield to vehicles coming from the right. If directly across, the car going straight has right-of-way over left turners. Check twice for crossing pedestrians who also have right-of-way.
When Merging
Drivers merging from a ramp or lane ending yield to traffic already on the highway. Adjust speed to find a gap rather than force your way into traffic. Be courteous and allow mergers to smoothly change lanes when possible.
In Roundabouts
Cars already in the roundabout have right-of-way. Use caution when entering, yielding to vehicles approaching from the left. Do not cut off cars already circling. Drive slowly and signal before exiting right.

For Pedestrians
Always yield right-of-way to pedestrians crossing roads, whether at crosswalks or uncontrolled intersections. Do not proceed until the pedestrian has fully cleared your lane. Watch for pedestrians still crossing if turning at intersections.
At Rail Crossings
Trains always have the right-of-way at rail crossings. Never attempt to drive around lowered gates or proceed until warning lights turn off and overpass barriers lift. Flashing lights indicate yield to any approaching trains.
For Emergency Vehicles
Immediately yield right-of-way when emergency vehicles approach from any direction with sirens blaring. Safely pull to the right side of the road and stop until the emergency vehicle passes. Do not block intersections that emergency responders need to access.
When Backing Up
Since rear view is limited while reversing, vehicles, pedestrians and cyclists already behind you have the right-of-way. Continually check backup camera displays and rear windows before slowly backing up. Stop immediately if anything crosses your path.
Mastering right-of-way rules prevents collisions at intersections, pedestrian crossings, and more. Always defer to others who have lawful permission to proceed first.

3.3 California Speed Limits

Speed limits exist to protect all roadway users. Driving at or below the posted speed limit allows proper control and reaction time to avoid collisions. California uses a basic speed law that requires safe driving at prudent speeds for conditions, even if below the limit. Know California-specific limits to stay safe and avoid costly speeding tickets.
Default Limits
When entering California roads with no posted limit signs, these default limits legally apply:

- 25 mph on most residential streets
- 55 mph on two-lane undivided highways
- 65 mph on multi-lane highways

Posted Limits
Watch for speed limit signs that override default limits on certain roads. Posted limits are set based on engineering studies considering

factors like design, safety, and traffic flow. Exceeding posted limits constitutes speeding in California.

Variable Limits

California utilizes electronic signs with variable speed limits that can change based on traffic conditions, weather, accidents, and construction zones. For example, limits may drop during peak congestion hours on highways to keep traffic moving smoothly. Adhere to digitally displayed limits that reflect current conditions.

Minimum Limits

On some highways, minimum 45 or 50 mph nighttime limits are posted to discourage unsafe slow driving. Carefully reduce speed if needed for safety, but avoid driving below minimums without justification or when the road allows higher speeds.

School Zones

School zones require reduced speed limits of 15-25 mph during posted hours to protect children. Passing a stopped school bus with flashing red lights is also prohibited. Fines double in school zones for traffic violations.

Construction Zones

Work zones require slower speeds for safety. Watch for and obey reduced limits marked on signs or on electronic message boards through active construction areas. Expect highway limits to drop to 45 mph or less.

Rain and Bad Weather

Basic speed law obligates drivers to slow during hazardous conditions like rain, fog, and snow. High speeds can lead to hydroplaning or skidding in wet weather. Visibility loss in fog demands lower speeds as well.

Curves and Exit Ramps

Sharp curves, uneven pavement, and exit ramps often have advisory speed signs. While not enforceable limits, these recommended speeds provide critical guidance for safely navigating tricky zones.

By learning the framework of California speed laws, you can confidently maintain safe, lawful speeds. Allow extra reaction time by moderating speeds for road environments and weather. The posted speed is not always the safe speed.

3.4 Parking Regulations and Restrictions

Finding lawful, safe parking requires understanding both general parking rules and specific restrictions. As a driver, you must comply with all posted parking limitations in California to avoid tickets, fines, towing, and blocking traffic. Master essential parking dos and don'ts.

Posted Time Limits

Many public parking spots have time limits restricting how long a vehicle can park there, usually noted on signs or curb markings. Be aware of 30 minute, 2-hour, 15-minute, etc. limits. Moving your car briefly does not restart the timer.

Restricted Zones

Watch for signage and colored curb markings that prohibit parking in certain areas 24/7. Common restricted zones include:

- Red curbs mean no stopping or parking for any reason.
- Blue curbs are for disabled permit holders only.
- Yellow and green curbs are short loading/unloading spaces.
- Fire hydrant areas and bus stop zones are off limits.

Permit Parking

In residential areas with permit parking only signs, vehicles must display local permits to legally park there. Permits do not override other posted restrictions. Visitors must find unrestricted parking nearby.

Parallel Parking

When roadside parking is allowed, vehicles must park parallel to the curb in the direction of traffic flow. Pull close to the curb and shift into reverse as needed to parallel park. Position within 12 inches of the curb.

No Parking Signs

Signs reading "No Parking" are enforced at all times. Do not stop or park for any reason in zones where parking prohibition signs are posted. This differs from "No Stopping/Standing" signs that forbid even brief waiting.

Park Completely

Avoid expensive parking tickets by pulling entirely within spaced lines and completely off streets. Double check sufficient clearance from corners, hydrants, driveways, and intersections.

Overnight Parking

Many cities ban street parking from 2-5am for street cleaning. Check for signage indicating overnight parking restrictions to avoid towing or fines.

Space Markers

Park only within designated space boundaries - do not take up multiple spaces. In unmarked areas, leave reasonable clearance between vehicles. Avoid oversized spots for compact cars only.

Disability Spaces

By law, only vehicles displaying valid disability placards/plates may use designated accessible parking spaces. Ilicit use brings huge fines.

Carefully reading and following all parking regulations protects you from penalties while keeping roads safely accessible. When in doubt, check signs or find an open, unrestricted space.

3.5 Understanding Traffic Lights and Signals

Traffic signal lights and signs play a vital role in controlling the orderly flow of vehicles, bicycles, and pedestrians. Obeying signals protects all road users by assigning right-of-way and regulating speed. Learn the meaning behind standard traffic light colors, arrows, and signs.

Solid Red Light

A steady circular red light at an intersection means come to a complete stop before first stopping lines or crosswalks. Wait for the light to turn green before legally proceeding straight or making any turn, unless turns on red are explicitly allowed after stopping. Never inch forward or anticipate the light changing.

Solid Yellow Light

A solid yellow traffic light indicates the signal is about to change to red. Slow down and prepare to make a safe, complete stop. Do not speed up to beat the red light. Continue through with caution if you are already in the intersection when the yellow appears.

Green Light

The green circular light signals permission to proceed straight through the intersection or make any legal turns after yielding to pedestrians and other vehicles already in the intersection. Left turns on green still require yielding to oncoming traffic.

Solid Green Arrow

A green arrow pointing left, right, or straight indicates you have the protected right-of-way to make only the turning movement shown by the arrow. Those with a red light must wait. Multiple green arrows authorize turns from dedicated lanes.

Flashing Yellow Arrow

This caution light allows turns after yielding to oncoming traffic and pedestrians. Vehicles approaching from the opposite direction still have the right-of-way until clear. Use judgment to turn safely without disrupting cross traffic flow.

Flashing Red Light

Treat flashing circular red lights the same as stop signs. Come to a full stop, check for crossing traffic and pedestrians, and proceed when clear. Turns on red may be allowed after a complete stop. Use caution at malfunctioning signals.

Pedestrian Signals

Obey pedestrian crossing signals at intersections, mid-block crosswalks, and school zones. Stop on red raised hands or "Don't Walk" signs. Yield to pedestrians when white "Walk" or green walking man symbols give them the go-ahead to cross.

Lane Use Signals

Arrows, Xs, and lines over lanes convey whether you must, can, or cannot drive in that lane. Position yourself in permitted lanes well in advance of intersections. Know whether lanes are dedicated turn only, straight only, or both.

By learning the meaning of all traffic lights and signs, you can drive confidently and safely through intersections. Signals provide order and prevent collisions when everyone reacts appropriately to them.

Chapter 4: Safe Driving Practices

4.1 The Importance of Safe Driving

Operating a vehicle is an enormous responsibility. Adopting safe driving practices protects you, your passengers, and everyone sharing the roads. While driving laws set the minimum standard, being a safe driver involves going above and beyond the basics. Committing to safety-first principles makes you not just a lawful driver, but an attentive, defensive driver as well.

The most fundamental advantage of safe driving is accident prevention. According to the National Highway Traffic Safety Administration, over 90% of crashes involve human error. Driving cautiously within speed limits, staying focused, and anticipating hazards drastically reduces your risks. Preventing accidents avoids injuries, deaths, legal issues, and financial costs for all parties involved.

Practicing safety also sets a positive example for others, especially young passengers and new drivers. Children learn driving behavior by observing you. Demonstrating safe habits you want copied gives them a priceless foundation. Teenagers are highly impressionable, so model responsible attitudes about risks and distractions.

Furthermore, diligent safety strengthens your skills as an alert, quick-thinking driver. Scanning 20-30 seconds ahead, regularly checking mirrors, and always signaling and checking blind spots sharpen your visual abilities and coordination. Defensive driving builds experience, confidence, and readiness to handle unexpected road events.

By driving safely, you earn the trust of passengers, pedestrians, and other motorists. They feel at ease knowing you are in control, paying attention, and looking out for them. This improves relationships and community goodwill. In return, others will show you courtesy as a fellow conscientious road user.

Most importantly, committing to safety demonstrates you value human life and wellbeing above all else. Whether family members or strangers, their safety is your responsibility behind the wheel. Patience and care for others must override frustration, anger, and schedule pressures. Prioritize safety over convenience or shaving minutes off your drive.

Driving is a long-term journey requiring daily safety mindfulness. Strive not just to be a lawful driver, but an attentive driver actively working to protect all lives on the road. Safe driving habits demonstrate prudence, maturity, and care for your passengers and community.

4.2 Defensive Driving Techniques

Defensive driving involves active awareness, caution, and strategic skills to prevent accidents in spite of hazards and mistakes of others. Master these key techniques to drive proactively instead of just reactively:

Scan Ahead Constantly

Look ahead 15-20 seconds to identify risks early, especially at intersections. Scan side to side, check mirrors every 5-8 seconds, and glance at instrument cluster gauges. Maintaining far sightlines allows time to plan avoidance maneuvers if needed.

Allow a Safe Following Distance

Leave a minimum 3-4 second following distance from the vehicle ahead at all speeds. This buffer zone gives you time to brake gradually and avoid tailgating collisions. Add more distance in poor conditions. If you pass a fixed object and reach it before 3 seconds elapse, drop back.

Cover the Brake

Keep your foot hovering gently over the brake pedal duringReady braking reduces reaction time. Covering the brake activates brake lights to alert others. Avoid riding or resting your foot on the brake which can lead to dangerous sudden braking.

Signal All Actions

Use turn signals for every turn, lane change, merge, and pull over well in advance so other drivers understand your intent. Signal even when you see no one nearby, as cars can quickly enter blind spots. Cancel signals once a maneuver is complete.

Decelerate Gradually

When slowing or stopping, avoid sudden, hard braking which can lead to skidding or loss of control. Gradually ease onto the brake pedal to give those behind you ample time to react. The slower the speed, the gentler the braking needs to be.

Leave Yourself an Out

In dense traffic, position your vehicle to have an escape path between lanes of traffic that allows evasive steering if needed. Monitor open lanes you could swerve into as a last resort to avoid collisions.

Drive Slowly in Bad Conditions

Reduce speed significantly during precipitation, fog, construction zones, and other hazards that limit visibility or traction. Turn lights

on, increase following distance, and stay well below the speed limit. Delay nonessential driving when roadways are dangerous.
Being a defensive driver requires full-time focus, caution, and diligence. But developing these habits and mindsets leads to a lifetime of accident-free driving.

4.3 Driving in Different Weather Conditions

Weather can greatly impact road conditions and vehicle control. As seasons change, you need to adjust driving to compensate for reduced traction, visibility, and stopping distance. Make safety the top priority in all weather by following smart precautions.
Rain
Water buildup causes slick roads, so begin braking early and slowly. Double the safe following distance to allow for longer stopping time. Turn on headlights so other drivers can see you. Avoid large water puddles and reduce speed through standing water to prevent hydroplaning where tires lose contact with the road.
Snow/Ice
Snow-covered or icy roads are extremely hazardous. Accelerate and brake gently to avoid skidding. Leave ample room between cars since stopping distance increases exponentially. Equip your vehicle with snow tires or chains for improved traction. Carry emergency supplies like blankets, flashlight, boots, etc.
Fog
Dense fog dramatically reduces visibility which is dangerous at high speeds. Slow down and use low beams rather than brights so the light refracts less through moisture droplets. Increase following distance to allow more reaction time. Pull aside and stop if the fog completely obscures vision.
High Winds
Maintain a strong grip on the wheel and reduce speed in strong crosswinds. Wind gusts can push vehicles out of a driving lane, especially lighter vehicles and high profile vehicles. Be prepared for sudden changes in conditions.
Nighttime
Visibility and depth perception diminish after dark. Drive with lights on low beam, and be alert for impaired night vision in your peripheral field. Reduce speed and increase following distance at night. Watch for pedestrians, cyclists, and animals who are harder to spot.
Bright Sun
Sun glare early or late in the day can temporarily blind drivers. Adjust the vehicle visors, wear sunglasses, and avoid looking directly into the

sun. Reduce speed until your vision sharpens. Be extra alert for hazards you may not see as quickly.
With smart preparation and defensive driving, weather does not need to prevent safe travel. Give yourself ample extra reaction time based on visibility and traction conditions. Prioritize safety over speed.

4.4 Dealing with Road Emergencies

Even the most safety-conscious drivers can unexpectedly face emergencies like blowouts, breakdowns, and crashes. While preventing problems is ideal, prepare for handling them calmly and safely if they do occur. Follow these tips to respond appropriately in roadside emergencies.
Remain Calm
Panic reduces your ability to think clearly and make wise choices. Take deep breaths and tell yourself you can handle this. Assess the situation and focus on deliberate next steps instead of speculating worst case scenarios. Being calm and rational helps resolve issues efficiently.
Pull Completely Off the Road
Get your disabled vehicle fully onto the shoulder, side street, or exit ramp to prevent getting hit by traffic. Turn on hazard lights immediately to alert other drivers. If unable to move your vehicle, get all passengers out and away from the road to prevent injuries.
Use Roadside Safety Tools
Many vehicles come equipped with tools to use in an emergency. Roadside safety kits contain flares, cones, reflectors, jump starter cables, first aid supplies, etc. Deploy these devices 10-70 feet behind your vehicle to alert oncoming traffic of the obstruction.
Contact Emergency Services
For collision injuries or dangerous roadway obstructions, call emergency services immediately. Give the exact incident location and a brief description of the problem. Dispatchers can send appropriate medical, police, and towing assistance.
Address Injuries
If an accident results in injuries, do not attempt to move victims unless the area becomes unstable or unsafe. Apply pressure to bleeding wounds with clean cloth. Keep the person still, warm, and as comfortable as possible until medical help arrives.
Try Minor Repairs
For minor breakdown issues, you may be able to perform temporary repairs yourself until permanent service can be scheduled. Change

belts/hoses, add fluids, replace wipers, etc. But do not make the vehicle operational unless fully safe to drive.
With the right preparation and clear decision making, road emergencies do not need to become catastrophic. Think through problems calmly, make the scene safe, and request help as appropriate.

4.5 Managing Distractions While Driving

Distracted driving due to phones, passengers, controls, or anything diverting attention is extremely dangerous and against the law in most states. As a driver, your top priority must always be focused attentiveness on the road and traffic conditions. Use smart tactics to identify and manage distractions.
Common Driving Distractions:

- Cell phones - texting, calls
- Loud passengers
- Technology screens - GPS, infotainment
- Controls - radio, heat/AC, wipers
- Eating, drinking, smoking
- Emotions - stress, anger, excitement
- Fatigue and drowsiness

Tips to Minimize Distractions:

- Silence phone notifications and calls or put on do not disturb mode
- Set navigation and music prior to driving
- Ask passengers to limit noise and movement
- Pull over safely to eat, program controls, calm emotions
- Take breaks on long drives when drowsy
- Keep eyes on the road instead of looking at passengers or devices
- Focus thoughts on driving tasks like scanning ahead

Avoid Multitasking s cannot truly multitask. Attempting to drive while focusing elsewhere divides attention and compromises coordinating skills vital to vehicle control. Refrain from any activity that competes for your visual, manual, or mental concentration.
Pull Over Safely
If a task must be done, like entering an address or quieting kids, pull completely off the road and stop first. Do not attempt while driving. Explain to passengers you are delaying activity for safety sake.
Minimize In-Vehicle Tech

The more vehicle screens and interactive tech features, the greater the distraction risk. Resist the urge to interact and set restrictions so passengers cannot become distracted either.

Mitigate Emotions

Anger, anxiety, sadness and excitement are proven distractions. Take deep breaths, play calming music, or talk through feelings to manage them before driving. Overwhelming emotions impair driving judgement.

Staying laser-focused on the driving environment, not internal thoughts or tasks, is the only way to prevent accidents. Make attentiveness your number one priority behind the wheel.

Chapter 5: Fines, Penalties, and Consequences

5.1 Importance of Knowing Fines and Penalties

Traffic offenses like speeding, DUI, and texting while driving carry legal consequences in every state. Learn the range of fines and penalties that apply to driving violations in your state. Understanding the financial, legal, and insurance impacts makes you think twice before disobeying traffic laws.

Traffic fines provide revenue for government budgets, but more importantly, they deter unlawful driving. Fines make you accountable for putting others in danger. Significantly increased fines for repeat offenses within 1-3 years further discourage illegal behavior behind the wheel.

Beyond base fine amounts, violation fees often get tacked on, which could include:

- Court fees
- Administrative fees
- Department of Motor Vehicles fees
- Driver education program fees
- Cost recovery surcharges

These extra penalties quickly multiply the actual fine you pay. Know the full costs before violating driving laws.

Serious traffic violations also result in license demerit points on your DMV record. Accumulating excessive points can trigger a license suspension or require completing traffic school. Multiple offenses within a short timeframe demonstrate negligence that could justify revoked driving privileges.

Criminal charges like reckless driving, street racing, or felony hit-and-run can lead to jail time. Lengthy incarcerations are possible when violations result in injury or death. Hiring legal representation becomes essential but quite costly if facing criminal prosecution.

Insurance rates increase an average of 30% for 3 years following a single moving violation like speeding. Multiple offenses within a few years can double your premiums. High rates will persist for 5+ years unless you complete defensive driving courses to help erase offenses from your record sooner.

Given the monetary burdens and personal consequences, it always pays to follow traffic rules. Driving safely within the law avoids fines, penalties, marksmans on your record, legal hassles and insurance rate hikes. Respect laws and drive responsibly.

5.2 Consequences of Traffic Violations

Beyond monetary fines, traffic violations can trigger far-reaching legal, administrative, and personal consequences for drivers. Understanding the cascading impacts of breaking traffic laws makes individuals think twice before taking risky actions behind the wheel.

License Points and Suspension

Most states assess demerit points on driving records for each violation like speeding, running red lights, and reckless driving. Points remain active 1-5 years depending on the state. Accumulating a set number within a 1-2 year timeframe - often 6-12 points - results in a suspended license.

Jail Time

Serious traffic offenses like DUI, vehicular manslaughter, or hit-and-run can lead to fines as well as months or years of jail time if convicted. Lengthy incarcerations are more likely when violations result in injuries or death due to negligence.

Fines and Fees

Base fine amounts for traffic violations quickly multiply once various fees get tacked on, including court fees, cost recovery fees, DMV fees, and more. The total outlay easily can exceed $500 for a single minor offense when all fines and fees are combined.

Insurance Rate Increases

Car insurance rates spike an average of 30% following just one violation like speeding or improper turning. Premiums often double after multiple offenses in 1-3 years. High rates persist for 3-5 years unless traffic school is completed to erase some violations.

Difficulty Finding Employment

Many employers conduct driver record background checks before hiring for jobs requiring driving. Multiple recent violations can eliminate you from consideration if driving is a primary duty.

Personal Trauma

When traffic offenses result in injury or death, drivers often experience overwhelming guilt, grief, post-traumatic stress, and health impacts that can persist for years. Negligent driving has deep human consequences beyond legal penalties.

License Reinstatement Difficulties

To regain a suspended license typically requires paying all original fines, re-applying for a license, retaking written and road exams, documenting insurance coverage, installing interlock devices, and other hurdles that take time and money to fulfill.

The cascading impact of traffic tickets, from fines to legal issues to job loss, demonstrates the importance of driving lawfully. Simple violations can trigger severe personal consequences. Making safe choices protects yourself and the public.

5.3 Understanding DUI and Its Penalties

Driving under the influence (DUI) of alcohol or drugs is illegal and highly dangerous. All states impose strict legal and financial penalties to deter drunk or drugged driving. Learn key facts about DUI laws and consequences to make responsible choices that keep yourself and the public safe.
What Constitutes DUI
Most states establish the illegal DUI blood alcohol content (BAC) threshold at .08%. Drivers 21+ with a BAC at or exceeding .08% commit DUI. For commercial drivers, the limit is lower at .04% BAC. Zero tolerance laws prohibit any detectable alcohol for drivers under 21. DUI also applies to driving impaired by marijuana, prescription medications, or illegal substances.
DUI Penalties
First offense DUIs typically incur fines of $500-$1000, with higher amounts for BAC levels over .15%. Jail sentences range from several days for misdemeanor DUI up to multiple years for felony DUI causing injuries or death. License suspension lasts 1-5 months for first offenses. Vehicles can be impounded and ignition interlock devices mandated.
Aggravated DUI Charges
Factors that elevate DUI to more severe criminal charges include:

- Extremely high BAC levels
- Repeat offenses within 5-10 years
- Speeding, reckless driving, hit-and-run associated with DUI
- Minor passengers present in the vehicle
- Injury or death caused by impaired driving

Long-Term Consequences
Beyond immediate DUI penalties, you face insurance rate hikes averaging $2,500 per year for 3+ years. Several offenses can make car insurance unattainable. DUIs remain on public records for 7-10 years, impacting job prospects and housing applications. Some states require ignition interlocks after multiple DUIs for up to 5 years.
Avoiding Trouble
Never drive after any alcohol consumption. Arrange alternate transportation like taxis, ride shares, public transit, or a designated driver. Eat while drinking to slow absorption. Stop drinking hours

before driving. Coffee cannot accelerate sobering up. Be sure prescribed medicine does not impair abilities before driving.
A DUI conviction creates legal headaches, financial burdens, driving restrictions, and public record challenges lasting for years. Drinking or drug use should always be fully separate from driving to keep the roads safe.

5.4 The Points System in California

California's point system is designed to hold dangerous drivers accountable through license suspension and revocation. DMV points remain active on your record for 3 years and accumulate with each traffic violation to potentially trigger serious repercussions. Know how DMV points impact your driving privileges.
Point Totals Per Violation
The number of points added to your California driving record varies by offense:

- 1 point - Minor offenses like broken taillight
- 2 points - Failures to appear, wear seat belts, properly restrain children
- 1-2 points - Most moving violations like speeding, illegal turns, stop sign/light violations
- 2 points - Accidents causing property damage
- 3-4 points - Reckless driving, passing violations
- 4 points - Speeding over 100 mph
- 6+ points - Felonies like vehicular manslaughter, street racing, or hit-and-run

License Suspension Triggers
Accumulating 4+ points in 12 months, 6+ points in 24 months, or 8+ points in 36 months results in a suspended license. Suspension lasts 1-3 months for first offenses, and up to a year for multiple offenses. License revocation requiring re-testing to reinstate is possible after multiple suspensions.
Under 21 Probation
Those under 21 face a 1 year license suspension after just 4 points in 12 months. They must prove good driving on a probationary license for 1 year before reinstatement to a full license.
Commercial License Impacts
Commercial drivers risk disqualification with 3 points in 12 months. A 60-150 day disqualification occurs at 4 points in 12 months, or 5-6 points in 24 months depending on the class of commercial vehicle driven.
Point Reduction Options

Completing traffic school allows 3 point reductions from the DMV record once every 18 months. Up to 7 points can be removed by a Driver's License Hearing or filing a Form DS 699 Request for Negligence Evaluation.
Given severity of suspensions and revocations, it is critical to maintain a clean driving record in California. Careful, lawful driving keeps points off your license.

5.5 How to Avoid Fines and Penalties

The most effective way to avoid traffic fines and penalties is to always drive lawfully and responsibly. But mistakes happen, so implement strategies to maintain a clean driving record. Minimizing violations protects your wallet, license status, and community safety.
Go the Speed Limit
Obeying posted speed limits eliminates one of the most common traffic citations. Allow extra drive time so you don't need to speed to appointments. Set cruise control to remember limits. Radar detectors can alert you to upcoming speed enforcement.
Come to Complete Stops
Runners who roll through stop signs and red lights are prone to tickets. Master full stops at intersections and behind limit lines or crosswalks. Scan all directions before proceeding. Teach new teen drivers the importance of full stops.
Be a Defensive Driver
Drive proactively, not just reactively, by scanning 20-30 seconds ahead and covering your brake. Defensive techniques like proper signaling and following distance give you more control to prevent violations.
Keep Vehicles Well Maintained
Ensure all vehicle equipment like headlights, turn signals, brake lights, and windshield wipers function properly to avoid fix-it tickets. Run down violations for unlit license plates, tinted windows, loud mufflers, and expired tags.
Park Legally
Read all parking signs carefully. Avoid illegal spots near hydrants, corners, driveways, or with time limits. Double check permitted parking hours to avoid overnight violations. Set reminders to plug meters.
Research Local Laws
Look up state and city statutes to learn the full scope of traffic, parking, and distracted driving laws. For example, codes detail fines

for littering, obstruction of license plates, unlawful tinting, noise violations, and other niche infractions.

Avoid Aggressive Driving

Steer clear of tailgating, speeding in traffic, unsafe lane changes, and gesturing/yelling. Road rage leads to reckless tickets and altercations. Take deep breaths and let frustrations go.

Eliminate Distractions

Don't text, program navigation, eat, or interact with rowdy passengers while driving. Safely pull over to handle any task diverting eyes and attention from the road.

With knowledge of laws and defensive habits, you can keep points off your license and avoid hefty fines. Safety is the priority, but prudent driving has monetary perks too.

Chapter 6: Questions and Answers with Detailed Explanations

Question 1: What does a red traffic light signify?
Answer: Stop.
Explanation: A red traffic light means you must come to a complete stop at the marked stop line or before moving into the crosswalk or intersection.
Question 2: What does a yellow traffic light mean?
Answer: Prepare to stop.
Explanation: A yellow traffic light means the signal is changing from green to red. Its purpose is to provide time for approaching vehicles to stop safely and to clear other vehicles from the intersection before the signal turns red.
Question 3: What does a flashing yellow traffic light mean?
Answer: Proceed with caution.
Explanation: A flashing yellow traffic light means you should slow down, yield to any pedestrians or vehicles in the intersection, and proceed with caution when it's safe to do so.
Question 4: What is the 'three-second rule'?
Answer: A method used to maintain a safe following distance at any speed.
Explanation: The 'three-second rule' helps you keep a safe distance from the vehicle in front of you while driving. You should keep at least 3 seconds of space between your vehicle and the vehicle in front of you.
Question 5: What should you do if an emergency vehicle is approaching while displaying flashing red lights, blue or white lights, and sounding a siren or bell?
Answer: Pull over to the right edge of the road and stop.
Explanation: When an emergency vehicle is approaching from either direction and displaying flashing lights or sounding a siren, all traffic should pull over to the right and stop until the emergency vehicle has passed.
Question 6: What is the speed limit in a school zone when children are present?
Answer: 25 mph, unless otherwise posted.
Explanation: The speed limit in a school zone when children are present is typically 25 mph. It can be lower, and when signs are posted, you should always follow the posted speed limit.
Question 7: What does a green arrow displayed on a traffic light mean?

Answer: You can proceed in the direction of the arrow.
Explanation: A green arrow means you can proceed in the direction of the arrow. If the red light is burning at the same time, you must be in the proper lane for such a turn and yield the right-of-way to vehicles and pedestrians within the intersection.
Question 8: When are you allowed to pass another vehicle on the right?
Answer: When the vehicle ahead is making a left turn, and there's enough room to pass.
Explanation: You may pass on the right of another vehicle making or about to make a left turn, if there is room to pass safely without driving off the roadway.
Question 9: What does a solid yellow line next to a broken yellow line mean?
Answer: You may pass if the broken line is on your side.
Explanation: This marking means that vehicles on the side with the broken line may pass when it is safe to do so, but vehicles on the side with the solid line may not.
Question 10: When can you make a left turn on red?
Answer: When turning from a one-way street onto another one-way street.
Explanation: A left turn on red is permitted when you are turning from a one-way street onto another one-way street, unless prohibited by a traffic sign.
Question 11: What does a "No U-Turn" sign mean?
Answer: U-turns are prohibited.
Explanation: The "No U-Turn" sign means you are prohibited from making a U-turn. You must not turn around to go in the opposite direction at this location.
Question 12: What does a "No Parking" sign mean?
Answer: Parking is not permitted.
Explanation: The "No Parking" sign means that you can't park your vehicle at specified locations or times. You can stop to load or unload merchandise or passengers though.
Question 13: When are you permitted to cross a double solid white line on the roadway?
Answer: You are not permitted to cross.
Explanation: Double solid white lines represent a barrier that you are not allowed to cross or pass. They are used to separate lanes of traffic moving in the same direction that you should not cross for any reason.
Question 14: What do you do if you approach an intersection with a non-operational traffic light?

Answer: Treat it as a four-way stop.
Explanation: If a traffic light is not working, you should treat the intersection as a four-way stop. The vehicle that arrived first has the right of way, and when vehicles arrive at roughly the same time, the vehicle on the right goes first.
Question 15: When must you yield to a transit bus in California?
Answer: When it signals and is pulling back onto the roadway.
Explanation: In California, you must yield to a transit bus pulling back onto the roadway when it has signaled its intention to do so.
Question 16: When driving in fog, you should use your:
Answer: Low beam headlights.
Explanation: When driving in fog, you should use your low beam headlights, not high beam, as high beams will reflect back off the fog and impair visibility even more.
Question 17: What does a flashing red traffic light mean?
Answer: Stop, yield the right-of-way, and proceed when it's safe.
Explanation: A flashing red light means the same as a STOP sign: Stop, yield the right-of-way to all approaching traffic and pedestrians, and then proceed when it's safe to do so.
Question 18: What is the appropriate action if you approach a roundabout, also known as a traffic circle?
Answer: Yield to drivers in the roundabout or traffic circle.
Explanation: When approaching a roundabout or traffic circle, drivers must yield to vehicles already in the circle, watch for pedestrians, and then proceed when it is safe to do so.
Question 19: What does a yellow diamond-shaped sign mean?
Answer: It's a warning sign.
Explanation: Yellow diamond signs are used to warn drivers about upcoming road conditions and hazards.
Question 20: When are you permitted to drive in the leftmost lane of a road with four or more lanes with two-way traffic?
Answer: When you are preparing for a left turn.
Explanation: On a road with four or more lanes with two-way traffic, you are permitted to drive in the leftmost lane when you are preparing for a left turn, or as permitted by traffic control signs.
Question 21: When are you allowed to drive on the shoulder of the road?
Answer: Only when directed to do so by a police officer or traffic control device.
Explanation: In general, driving on the shoulder is prohibited. You should only drive on the shoulder if a police officer or traffic control device (sign, signal, or road marking) directs you to do so.

Question 22: What should you do if your car begins to skid?
Answer: Steer in the direction you want the vehicle to go and ease off the gas.
Explanation: If your vehicle begins to skid, you should remain calm, steer in the direction you want the vehicle to go, ease off the gas, and avoid slamming on the brakes, which could upset the vehicle's balance and make it harder to control.
Question 23: What is the legal limit of blood alcohol concentration (BAC) for drivers 21 years and older?
Answer: 0.08%
Explanation: The legal limit of blood alcohol concentration (BAC) for drivers aged 21 and older is 0.08%. However, drivers can be arrested for driving under the influence (DUI) with lower BAC if their driving is impaired.
Question 24: What should you do if you approach a school bus with flashing red lights?
Answer: Stop.
Explanation: If you approach a school bus with flashing red lights, you must stop from either direction until the lights stop flashing. The flashing red lights mean children are entering or leaving the bus.
Question 25: What should you do when you hear a siren coming from behind your vehicle?
Answer: Pull over to the right edge of the road and stop.
Explanation: When you hear a siren or see a vehicle approaching from behind with flashing lights, you should pull over to the right edge of the road and stop. This allows emergency vehicles to pass you on the left.
Question 26: Who has the right of way when two vehicles arrive at an intersection at the same time?
Answer: The vehicle on the right.
Explanation: At an intersection where there is no stop sign, yield sign, or oncoming traffic signal, vehicles must yield to vehicles from the right.
Question 27: What is the hand signal for a left turn?
Answer: Arm straight out.
Explanation: The hand signal for a left turn is to extend your arm straight out from the side of your vehicle.
Question 28: What does a "Slippery When Wet" sign mean?
Answer: The road may be especially slick and dangerous when wet or rainy.
Explanation: A "Slippery When Wet" sign is often located before bridges or shaded areas where the road may become particularly

dangerous when it's wet or raining. Drivers should slow down and use caution when they see these signs.

Question 29: What should you do if an emergency vehicle with flashing lights is directly behind your vehicle in heavy traffic?

Answer: Keep moving slowly until you can get out of the way.

Explanation: If an emergency vehicle with flashing lights is directly behind your vehicle in heavy traffic, keep moving as best you can until you're able to safely move to the side of the road and come to a stop.

Question 30: What should you do if your vehicle's right wheels drift off the pavement?

Answer: Take your foot off the accelerator and steer in the direction you want to go when it's safe.

Explanation: If your vehicle's right wheels drift off the pavement, don't try to turn back onto the pavement right away. Instead, reduce your speed by taking your foot off the accelerator and steer in the direction you want to go. When it's safe, turn the steering wheel to go back onto the pavement at a low speed.

Question 31: Which way should your car face when parked uphill next to a curb?

Answer: Away from the curb.

Explanation: When parked uphill next to a curb, the vehicle should be turned away from the curb. This way, if it rolls, it will roll into the curb and stop.

Question 32: What does a "Yield" sign mean?

Answer: Give the right of way to other road users.

Explanation: A "Yield" sign means you must give the right of way to the traffic on the road you're entering or crossing.

Question 33: What should you do before backing up your vehicle?

Answer: Check your mirrors and look over your shoulder.

Explanation: Before backing up, you should check all mirrors and look over your right shoulder to check the blind spots. This allows you to see any vehicles, people, or obstacles in your path.

Question 34: What does a "Slow Down" sign mean?

Answer: Decrease your speed.

Explanation: A "Slow Down" sign is a regulatory sign that indicates drivers must lower their speed in the area ahead due to road conditions or other safety concerns.

Question 35: Can you use a handheld cell phone while driving?

Answer: No.

Explanation: Using a handheld cell phone while driving is illegal in many jurisdictions due to the associated distractions and risks. It's

important to use hands-free options or pull over safely if you need to make a call.
Question 36: What does a white line across your lane at an intersection indicate?
Answer: The location where you should stop.
Explanation: A white stop line painted across a lane at an intersection indicates where you should stop your vehicle. If a traffic signal or officer directs you to stop, you should stop before the white line.
Question 37: What should you do if a police officer signals you to pull over?
Answer: Safely pull over to the side of the road and come to a complete stop.
Explanation: If a police officer signals you to pull over, you should promptly but safely move your vehicle to the side of the road and come to a complete stop in a safe place.
Question 38: What does a flashing yellow arrow signal mean?
Answer: You may proceed with the turn but must yield to oncoming traffic.
Explanation: A flashing yellow arrow signal indicates that you are allowed to make a turn in the direction of the arrow, but you must yield to opposing traffic or pedestrians who have a green light.
Question 39: What should you do if you encounter an aggressive driver?
Answer: Keep your distance and avoid making eye contact or gestures.
Explanation: If you encounter an aggressive driver, it's important to keep your distance, avoid making eye contact or gestures, and not challenge them. If you feel threatened, call the police.
Question 40: What does a "Pedestrian Crossing" sign mean?
Answer: Watch for people crossing the road.
Explanation: A "Pedestrian Crossing" sign warns drivers to expect pedestrians and to yield to them as they cross the road.
Question 41: What is a crosswalk?
Answer: A part of the roadway set aside for pedestrian traffic.
Explanation: A crosswalk is a part of the roadway set aside for pedestrians to cross. It may be marked by white lines or may be unmarked.
Question 42: What is the basic speed law?
Answer: Never drive faster than is safe for current conditions.
Explanation: The basic speed law dictates that you should never drive faster than is safe for the current conditions, regardless of the posted speed limit.

Question 43: What should you do if your vehicle starts to hydroplane?
Answer: Ease off the accelerator and steer in the direction you want to go.
Explanation: If your vehicle starts to hydroplane, ease off the accelerator but do not brake abruptly. Keep a firm grip on the steering wheel and steer in the direction you want to go.
Question 44: What is the penalty for driving under the influence of alcohol or drugs?
Answer: Penalties include fines, imprisonment, and/or loss of driving privilege.
Explanation: Penalties for driving under the influence of alcohol or drugs can be severe, including hefty fines, imprisonment, loss of driving privileges, and mandatory alcohol or drug education programs.
Question 45: When is it legal to use your horn?
Answer: When it may help prevent an accident.
Explanation: It's legal to use your horn when you need to attract another driver's attention to prevent46. **Question 46:** What are guide signs?
Answer: Signs that provide information about roadways and routes.
Explanation: Guide signs are designed to provide information to assist motorists in navigating to their destination. They can indicate route numbers, distances, directions, and points of interest.
Question 47: When can you cross a double solid yellow line?
Answer: When making a turn into a driveway.
Explanation: A double solid yellow line indicates that passing or changing lanes is not allowed in either direction. You may cross these lines only to turn left into a driveway or alley.
Question 48: What should you do when approaching a roundabout?
Answer: Yield to traffic already in the roundabout and then proceed when it is safe.
Explanation: When approaching a roundabout, you should yield to the traffic already in the roundabout. Once you see a gap in traffic, enter the roundabout and proceed to your exit.
Question 49: What should you do if a traffic signal is not working at an intersection?
Answer: Treat the intersection as a four-way stop.
Explanation: If a traffic signal is not working at an intersection, you should treat the intersection as a four-way stop. This means that the first vehicle to stop at the intersection has the right of way

and may proceed first. If two vehicles arrive at the same time, the vehicle on the right goes first.
Question 50: What should you do if you are involved in a car accident?
Answer: Stop your vehicle at or near the collision scene, but do not obstruct traffic. Assist anyone injured, exchange information with other parties involved, and notify the police.
Explanation: If you are involved in a car accident, it's important to stop your vehicle at or near the collision scene without obstructing traffic. Check for injuries and call for help if needed. Exchange name, address, driver's license number, vehicle registration, and insurance information with the other party. Report the accident to the police, even if it's minor.
Question 51: What is defensive driving?
Answer: Driving to prevent accidents in spite of the incorrect actions of others.
Explanation: Defensive driving involves anticipating dangerous situations and preparing responses in advance. It means driving to prevent accidents regardless of the actions of other drivers or the presence of adverse driving conditions.
Question 52: What is the difference between a divided and undivided roadway?
Answer: A divided roadway has a physical barrier between traffic moving in opposite directions, while an undivided roadway does not.
Explanation: A divided roadway has a median or barrier that separates traffic moving in opposite directions. In contrast, traffic moves in opposite directions separated by only a lane marking on an undivided roadway.
Question 53: What should you do when driving in foggy conditions?
Answer: Slow down, use your low-beam headlights, and maintain a safe following distance.
Explanation: When driving in fog, you should slow down, use your low-beam headlights (not high-beams, as they can reflect off the fog and reduce visibility), and increase your following distance to ensure you have enough time to react to hazards.
Question 54: What should you do if a law enforcement officer is directing traffic at a traffic signal?
Answer: Follow the directions of the officer.
Explanation: If a law enforcement officer is directing traffic at a traffic signal, you should follow the officer's directions, even if they contradict the traffic signal.

Question 55: What does a red and white triangular sign at an intersection mean?
Answer: "Yield" - You must let all traffic and pedestrians near you go before you proceed.
Explanation: A red and white triangular sign at an intersection is a "Yield" sign. You must slow down or stop if necessary so that you can yield the right-of-way to pedestrians and vehicles.
Question 56: What should you do if your accelerator sticks while you are driving?
Answer: Shift to neutral, apply the brakes, look for a safe way out, and turn off the engine when you are safely off the road.
Explanation: If your accelerator sticks, stay calm and follow these steps: Shift your vehicle to neutral. Apply the brakes to slow your vehicle. Look for a safe way off the road. Once you are off the road, turn off your engine.
Question 57: What are rumble strips?
Answer: Rumble strips are a road safety feature to alert inattentive drivers of potential danger, by causing a tactile vibration and audible rumbling.
Explanation: Rumble strips are placed on the roadway to alert drivers.
Question 58: What is the hand signal for a left turn?
Answer: Extend your arm straight out from your side.
Explanation: To indicate a left turn using hand signals, you should extend your left arm straight out from your side.
Question 59: What should you do if you miss your exit on a highway?
Answer: Continue to the next exit.
Explanation: If you miss your exit on a highway, do not stop or back up. Instead, you should continue on to the next exit.
Question 60: What should you do if a traffic signal turns yellow as you approach an intersection?
Answer: Stop if it is safe to do so.
Explanation: If the traffic signal turns yellow as you approach an intersection, you should stop if it is safe to do so. If you are too close to the intersection to stop safely, you should continue through the intersection with caution.
Question 61: What should you do if your vehicle breaks down on a highway?
Answer: Pull off the road as far as possible, turn on your hazard lights, and call for help.
Explanation: If your vehicle breaks down on a highway, you should pull off the road as far as possible, preferably into the

breakdown lane if one is available. Turn on your hazard lights to alert other drivers, and call for help.
Question 62: What does a flashing red traffic signal mean?
Answer: Stop, then proceed when it is safe to do so.
Explanation: A flashing red traffic signal has the same meaning as a stop sign. You should come to a complete stop, then proceed when it is safe and legal to do so.
Question 63: What is the proper way to enter a highway from the entrance ramp?
Answer: Use the entrance ramp and acceleration lane to increase your speed to match the flow of traffic, then merge safely.
Explanation: When entering a highway, you should use the entrance ramp and acceleration lane to increase your speed to match the flow of traffic on the highway. You should signal and check for a gap in the traffic, then merge safely into the flow of traffic.
Question 64: What should you do if you encounter a school bus with its red lights flashing?
Answer: Stop.
Explanation: If you encounter a school bus with its red lights flashing, you must stop. This indicates that children are getting on or off the school bus, and you must not pass the bus.
Question 65: What is a safe following distance under normal driving conditions?
Answer: 2 seconds.
Explanation: Under normal driving conditions, you should maintain at least a 2-second distance between your vehicle and the vehicle ahead. This distance should be increased in adverse weather conditions or when following large vehicles.
Question 66: What is the correct response to a solid yellow traffic signal?
Answer: Stop if it's safe to do so.
Explanation: A solid yellow traffic signal indicates that the light is about to turn red. You should stop if it is safe to do so. If you are too close to the intersection to stop safely, continue carefully through the intersection.
Question 67: When is it legal to pass another vehicle using the shoulder of the road?
Answer: It is never legal.
Explanation: Passing another vehicle using the shoulder of the road is dangerous and generally illegal. You should only use the shoulder for emergencies.

Question 68: When is it necessary to use your headlights during daylight hours?
Answer: When visibility is poor due to weather conditions.
Explanation: You should use your headlights during daylight hours when visibility is poor due to weather conditions such as rain, snow, fog, or dust.
Question 69: What does a "No Passing Zone" sign mean?
Answer: It's not safe or legal to pass another vehicle.
Explanation: A "No Passing Zone" sign is posted where it is unsafe and illegal to pass another vehicle, such as in a curve or near a hillcrest.
Question 70: What does a green arrow displayed on a traffic signal mean?
Answer: You are permitted to drive in the direction of the arrow.
Explanation: A green arrow displayed on a traffic signal indicates that you are permitted to drive in the direction of the arrow, and that oncoming traffic is stopped by a red light.
Question 71: What should you do if you are driving and become tired or fatigued?
Answer: Pull over in a safe place and rest.
Explanation: If you are driving and become tired or fatigued, you should pull over in a safe place and rest. Driving while fatigued can72. **Question 72:** What should you do if your car begins to skid?
Answer: Steer in the direction you want the vehicle to go and ease off the gas pedal.
Explanation: If your vehicle begins to skid, you should remain calm, ease your foot off the gas, and carefully steer in the direction you want the front of the vehicle to go.
Question 73: What does a solid white line on the road indicate?
Answer: You should stay within your lane and crossing it is discouraged.
Explanation: A solid white line on the road indicates that lane changes are discouraged due to potential dangers.
Question 74: What is the most important thing to do before changing lanes?
Answer: Check your mirrors and blind spots.
Explanation: Before changing lanes, it's crucial to check your mirrors and blind spots to ensure there are no vehicles in the lane you wish to enter.
Question 75: How should you react to an approaching emergency vehicle with its lights and siren on?
Answer: Pull to the side of the road and stop.

Explanation: When an emergency vehicle is approaching with its lights and siren on, you should safely pull over to the side of the road and stop.
Question 76: What does a flashing yellow light mean at an intersection?
Answer: Proceed with caution.
Explanation: A flashing yellow light at an intersection means that you should slow down and proceed with caution, yielding to any vehicles or pedestrians in the intersection.
Question 77: What should you do if a police officer signals for you to pull over?
Answer: Safely pull over to the side of the road and stop.
Explanation: If a police officer signals for you to pull over, you should safely pull over to the side of the road as soon as possible, turn off your engine, and wait for the officer to approach your vehicle.
Question 78: When are you allowed to drive in a bicycle lane?
Answer: Only when turning, entering or leaving the roadway, or when parking where parking is permitted.
Explanation: Driving in a bicycle lane is generally prohibited. However, you may enter a bicycle lane for the purpose of making a turn, entering or leaving the roadway, or when parking where parking is permitted.
Question 79: What should you do if your vehicle starts to hydroplane?
Answer: Ease off the accelerator and steer in the direction you want to go.
Explanation: If your vehicle starts to hydroplane (slide on the water on the road), you should ease off the accelerator, avoid hard braking or turning sharply, and steer in the direction that the front of your vehicle needs to go.
Question 80: What is the first thing you should do if your accelerator sticks while you're driving?
Answer: Shift to neutral and use the brakes to slow your vehicle.
Explanation: If your accelerator sticks while you're driving, you should shift to neutral, apply the brakes to slow your vehicle, look for a safe way out, and turn off the ignition when you're safely off the road.
Question 81: What is the "three-second rule"?
Answer: It's a guide to ensure you're leaving enough space between your vehicle and the vehicle in front.
Explanation: The "three-second rule" helps you determine a safe following distance. Choose a fixed point that is even with the car in

front of you. If you reach that same fixed point before you can count to three, then you are driving too close to the vehicle in front of you and should reduce your speed.
Question 82: Why should you avoid driving in other drivers' blind spots?
Answer: Because the other driver may not see you and could change lanes into you.
Explanation: You should avoid driving in other drivers' blind spots because they may not see your vehicle. Always try to position your vehicle where it can be seen.
Question 83: What should you do if the car behind you is following too closely?
Answer: Slow down and allow them to pass, or pull over and let them go by.
Explanation: If the car behind you is following too closely, you should signal and pull over when it's safe to do so to let them pass. If this is not possible, slow down slightly to encourage them to pass.
Question 84: What should you do if you're approaching a green light that's been green for a long time?
Answer: Be prepared to stop, the light is likely about to change to yellow.
Explanation: If you're approaching a green light that's been green for a long time, this is known as a "stale" green light, and it's likely to turn yellow soon.
Question 85: What does a double yellow line on the road indicate?
Answer: No passing is allowed from either direction.
Explanation: A double yellow line in the middle of the road means that passing is not allowed from either direction. You should not cross these lines unless you are turning left when it is safe to do so.
Question 86: What should you do if your vehicle's right wheels drift off onto the shoulder of the road?
Answer: Take your foot off the gas and steer parallel to the road. Once the right wheels are back on the pavement, steer back onto the roadway.
Explanation: If your vehicle's right wheels drift onto the shoulder of the road, you should take your foot off the gas and steer straight ahead parallel to the road. When the right wheels have regained traction, steer back onto the roadway. Do not try to jerk the vehicle back onto the pavement as this could cause loss of control.
Question 87: When are roads most likely to be slippery?
Answer: Just after it has started to rain.

Explanation: Roads are most slippery just after it has started to rain. Oil and dust have not been washed away yet and create a slick layer on the road surface.
Question 88: When is it illegal to use your horn?
Answer: In residential areas or city streets late at night or early in the morning.
Explanation: It is generally illegal to use your horn in residential areas or city streets late at night or early in the morning, except in an emergency situation.
Question 89: How should you adjust your driving in construction zones?
Answer: Slow down, obey all signs and signals, and be prepared for unexpected changes in the roadway.
Explanation: When driving in construction zones, you should slow down and obey all signs and signals. Be prepared for unexpected changes in the roadway, such as narrowed lanes or detours.
Question 90: When should you signal for a turn?
Answer: At least 100 feet before the intersection.
Explanation: You should signal for a turn at least 100 feet before the intersection. If you are on a highway, you should signal at least 500 feet before the turn.
Question 91: What is the legal blood alcohol concentration (BAC) limit for drivers over 21 in most states?
Answer: 0.08%.
Explanation: In most states, the legal blood alcohol concentration (BAC) limit for drivers over 21 is 0.08%. However, drivers can be arrested for impaired driving even with a lower BAC.
Question 92: What should you do if you approach an intersection where the traffic lights are not working?
Answer: Treat it as a four-way stop.
Explanation: If you approach an intersection where the traffic lights are not working, you should treat it as a four-way stop. That means you must stop at the intersection and then proceed when it is your turn.
Question 93: When is it acceptable to use your emergency brake?
Answer: When your primary braking system fails.
Explanation: The emergency brake, also known as the parking brake, should be used when your primary braking system fails. It can also be used when parking, especially on a hill.
Question 94: What is the best way to prevent skidding on slippery surfaces?
Answer: Slow down and increase your following distance.
Explanation: The best way to prevent skidding on slippery

surfaces is to slow down and increase your following distance. You should also avoid sudden braking, acceleration, or turns.
Question 95: When is it safe to return to the right-hand lane after passing a vehicle on the left?
Answer: When you can see the passed vehicle's headlights in your rear-view mirror.
Explanation: It is safe to return to the right-hand lane after passing a vehicle on the left when you can see the passed vehicle's headlights in your rear-view mirror.
Question 96: What is the minimum safe distance you should keep from a bicyclist when passing?
Answer: Three feet.
Explanation: When passing a bicyclist, you should keep a minimum distance of three feet between your vehicle and the bicycle.
Question 97: What should you do if you encounter a dust storm while driving?
Answer: Pull over safely off the roadway, turn off your lights, and wait for the storm to pass.
Explanation: If you encounter a dust storm while driving, you should pull over safely off the roadway, turn off your lights, and wait for the storm to pass. Turning off your lights will prevent other drivers from mistakenly following you, thinking you are on the road.
Question98: What should you do if you are involved in a collision?
Answer: Stop your vehicle at or near the collision scene without obstructing traffic, exchange information with other involved parties and report the incident to the police.
Explanation: If you are involved in a collision, you should stop your vehicle without obstructing traffic, if possible. You must provide your name, address, and vehicle registration number to the other parties involved. If someone is injured, you should also do what you can to provide assistance, and you must report the collision to the police.
Question 99: What does a flashing red traffic light signal mean?
Answer: Stop, yield to traffic and pedestrians, and proceed when it's safe.
Explanation: A flashing red traffic light signal means the same as a stop sign: you must come to a complete stop, yield to traffic and pedestrians, and proceed when it's safe.
Question 100: What is the purpose of rumble strips on the roadway?
Answer: To alert inattentive drivers through vibration and sound

that they are approaching a hazard or leaving the roadway.
Explanation: Rumble strips are usually placed on the edges of the roadway or on the centerline. They create a vibration and loud rumbling noise when driven over, which hèlps to alert inattentive drivers that they are approaching a hazard or leaving the roadway.
Question 101: What is the "three-second rule" in driving?
Answer: The three-second rule is a guideline for safe following distance. Choose a fixed point ahead, when the vehicle ahead passes it, count "one thousand one, one thousand two, one thousand three". If you pass the point before finishing the count, you're too close.
Explanation: The three-second rule helps to maintain a safe distance between your car and the vehicle in front of you. It's especially important in bad weather conditions or at high speeds, when the stopping distance is increased.
Question 102: What is the most common cause of crashes?
Answer: Distracted driving.
Explanation: Distracted driving, which includes texting, talking on the phone, eating, or using in-car technologies, is the most common cause of road crashes.
Question 103: Why should you avoid driving in the blind spots of other vehicles?
Answer: Because the other driver may not see you and could change lanes or make other maneuvers, causing a collision.
Explanation: Blind spots are areas around a vehicle that the driver can't see in their mirrors. If you're driving in another vehicle's blind spot, the driver may not be aware of your presence, which increases the risk of a collision.
Question 104: When is it okay to pass on the right?
Answer: When you're on a road with two or more lanes traveling in the same direction or the vehicle in front of you is making a left turn and you do not have to leave the paved road to pass.
Explanation: Passing on the right is generally allowed when the road has two or more lanes traveling in the same direction, or when the vehicle in front of you is making a left turn and you can pass without leaving the paved road. However, it's important to always check local traffic laws.
Question 105: What should you do if your car starts to hydroplane?
Answer: Ease off the accelerator, do not make sudden turns, and allow the car to slow until the tires regain traction.
Explanation: Hydroplaning occurs when a layer of water comes between your tires and the road, causing the car to skid or slide. If

this happens, the best thing to do is to ease off the accelerator, avoid sudden turns or hard braking, and allow the car to slow down until the tires regain traction with the road surface.
Question 106: What is the purpose of an acceleration lane?
Answer: Acceleration lanes are used to increase your vehicle speed to match that of the highway traffic before merging.
Explanation: Acceleration lanes are found on the entrance of highways and are used to help vehicles safely reach the speed of other vehicles on the highway before they merge onto it.
Question 107: When should high-beam headlights be used?
Answer: In rural areas or on unfamiliar roads, in conditions of rain, fog, snow, or smoke, or when there are no oncoming vehicles within 500 feet.
Explanation: High-beam headlights provide stronger illumination than low-beams and can be used for better visibility in rural or unfamiliar areas and in certain weather conditions. However, they should not be used when other vehicles are within 500 feet, as the strong light can blind other drivers.
Question 108: What should you do if your car breaks down on the highway?
Answer: Safely pull off the road, turn on your hazard lights, and call for help.
Explanation: If your car breaks down on the highway, you should safely pull off the road as far as possible to avoid obstructing traffic. Turn on your hazard lights to alert other drivers, and call for roadside assistance or a tow truck.
Question 109: What is the purpose of a deceleration lane?
Answer: Deceleration lanes are used to slow down your vehicle speed before exiting a highway.
Explanation: Deceleration lanes are found at highway exits and are used to help vehicles safely decrease their speed before leaving the highway.
Question 110: What should you do if you approach a school bus with its lights flashing and stop arm extended?
Answer: Stop and wait until the lights stop flashing and the stop arm is withdrawn before proceeding.
Explanation: If you approach a school bus with its lights flashing and stop arm extended, you should stop and wait. This indicates that children are getting on or off the bus, and it's illegal in all 50 states to pass a school bus in this situation.
Question 111: How should you respond to an approaching emergency vehicle with its lights and siren on?
Answer: Pull over to the right side of the road and stop until the

emergency vehicle has passed.
Explanation: When an emergency vehicle with its lights and siren on is approaching, you should pull over to the right side of the road and stop until the vehicle has passed. This allows emergency vehicles to reach their destinations as quickly as possible.
Question 112: What does a solid white line on the road indicate?
Answer: You should stay within your lane and it also marks the shoulder of the roadway.
Explanation: A solid white line on the road indicates that lane changes are discouraged, and you should stay within your lane. A solid white line also marks the shoulder of the roadway.
Question 113: What do orange-colored signs on the highway usually represent?
Answer: Construction and maintenance warning.
Explanation: Orange-colored signs on the highway usually represent temporary traffic control due to construction and maintenance activities. They are used to warn drivers of potential dangers and to guide them safely through the work zone.
Question 114: What is the legal driving age in most states in the U.S.?
Answer: 16 years old.
Explanation: In most states in the U.S., the legal age to obtain a driver's license is 16 years old. However, this can vary by state, and many states have graduated driver's licensing programs that allow for supervised driving at younger ages.
Question 115: What is a roundabout?
Answer: A roundabout is a circular intersection where traffic flows around a central island.
Explanation: Roundabouts are designed to improve safety by slowing traffic speeds and reducing conflict points where crashes can occur. Vehicles entering the roundabout must yield to traffic already in the circle.
Question 116: What should you do if you miss your exit on a highway?
Answer: Continue to the next exit.
Explanation: If you miss your exit on a highway, you should continue to the next exit. It is dangerous and usually illegal to back up or try to turn around on a highway.
Question 117: What is the difference between a controlled and uncontrolled intersection?
Answer: A controlled intersection has traffic signals or signs. An uncontrolled intersection has no signs or signals.
Explanation: At a controlled intersection, traffic signals or signs

dictate the flow of traffic. At an uncontrolled intersection, there are no signs or signals, and drivers must yield to traffic on the right and to any vehicles already in the intersection.
Question 118: What does it mean if a pedestrian is carrying a white cane or using a guide dog?
Answer: The pedestrian is visually impaired or blind.
Explanation: Pedestrians who are visually impaired or blind often use a white cane or a guide dog to help them navigate. Drivers should yield the right-of-way to these pedestrians.
Question 119: What does a green arrow signal mean at a traffic light?
Answer: You may proceed in the direction of the arrow, if you are in the correct lane.
Explanation: A green arrow signal at a traffic light means you may proceed in the direction of the arrow, if you are in the correct lane. This is often used to control turns at intersections.
Question 120: What should you do if you are involved in a minor traffic collision with no injuries?
Answer: Move your vehicle out of traffic, if possible, **Explanation:** If you are involved in a minor traffic collision and there are no injuries, you should try to move your vehicle out of traffic to a safe location to prevent further accidents, and then exchange information with the other driver. You should also report the collision to the police and your insurance company.
Question 121: What is the term for driving under the influence of alcohol or drugs?
Answer: DUI (Driving Under the Influence) or DWI (Driving While Intoxicated)
Explanation: DUI and DWI are terms used to refer to the illegal act of driving a vehicle while impaired by alcohol or other drugs, including recreational and prescribed drugs.
Question 122: What is the fast lane on a highway?
Answer: The fast lane, often the lane furthest to the left, is generally used for passing other vehicles.
Explanation: On a multi-lane road, the "fast lane" or "passing lane" is typically the lane furthest to the left (in countries where driving is on the right side of the road). It's intended for vehicles to overtake slower traffic.
Question 123: What should you do if your vehicle starts to skid?
Answer: Steer in the direction you want the front of your vehicle to go, ease off the gas, and carefully apply the brakes if you have anti-lock brakes.
Explanation: If your vehicle starts to skid, stay calm, ease your

foot off the gas, and carefully steer in the direction you want the front of your vehicle to go. If you have standard brakes, pump them gently; if you have anti-lock brakes (ABS), do not pump the brakes, but apply steady pressure instead.
Question 124: What is a blind spot in driving?
Answer: A blind spot is an area around your vehicle that cannot be directly observed while looking forward or through either the rear-view or side mirrors.
Explanation: A blind spot in driving refers to the area around your vehicle that is not visible in your mirrors or peripheral vision. It's important to check these blind spots by turning your head and looking over your shoulder before changing lanes or merging.
Question 125: What does a flashing yellow traffic light mean?
Answer: Proceed with caution.
Explanation: A flashing yellow traffic light is a warning that the signal is "unprotected" and oncoming traffic may not be required to stop. Drivers should slow down, look for other traffic, and proceed with caution.
Question 126: What should you do if you're involved in a hit-and-run accident?
Answer: Try to remember as many details as possible about the other vehicle and driver, report the incident to the police, and contact your insurance company.
Explanation: If you're involved in a hit-and-run accident, it's important to try to remember as many details as possible about the other vehicle and driver, such as the license plate number, make and model of the car, and a description of the driver. You should report the incident to the police as soon as possible, and also notify your insurance company.
Question 127: What should you do if your vehicle's engine overheats?
Answer: Pull over safely, turn off the engine, and wait for it to cool down before checking the coolant level.
Explanation: If your vehicle's engine overheats, you should pull over safely as soon as possible and turn off the engine. Once it's cooled down, check the coolant level and add more if necessary. If the problem persists, you might need to get the vehicle towed and inspected by a mechanic.
Question 128: What does a red octagonal sign usually signify?
Answer: Stop.
Explanation: A red octagonal sign is a stop sign. It means that drivers must come to a complete stop before proceeding.

Question 129: What is the purpose of a rumble strip?
Answer: To alert inattentive drivers of potential danger.
Explanation: Rumble strips are a road safety feature that causes a vehicle to vibrate and produce a loud rumbling sound when the tires come into contact with them. They are usually installed on the edges of roads or on the centerline to alert inattentive drivers that they are drifting out of their lane or approaching a stop sign or signal.
Question 130: What do you do if your brakes fail while driving?
Answer: Pump the brake pedal rapidly; if that doesn't work, use the parking brake while holding the release button, and shift to a lower gear if possible.
Explanation: If your brakes fail while driving, first try pumping the brake pedal rapidly to build up brake fluid pressure. If that doesn't work, you can use the parking brake - hold the release button to modulate the brake pressure and prevent skidding.
Question 131: What does a yellow diamond-shaped sign indicate?
Answer: Warning.
Explanation: Yellow diamond-shaped signs are warning signs. They are used to warn drivers of upcoming hazards or changes in road conditions.
Question 132: What does a double yellow line in the center of the road signify?
Answer: No passing.
Explanation: A double yellow line in the center of the road signifies that passing is not allowed for vehicles traveling in either direction.
Question 133: What is the purpose of a median on a highway?
Answer: To separate traffic moving in opposite directions.
Explanation: A median on a highway is used to separate traffic moving in opposite directions. This can help prevent head-on collisions and can provide a safe area for emergency vehicles.
Question 134: What should you do if your vehicle starts to hydroplane?
Answer: Ease off the accelerator and steer in the direction you want to go.
Explanation: Hydroplaning occurs when a layer of water builds up between your vehicle's tires and the road surface, causing the vehicle to lose traction. If your vehicle starts to hydroplane, you should ease off the accelerator and steer in the direction you want to go. Do not brake or turn suddenly as this could cause a skid.
Question 135: What is the purpose of a turn signal?
Answer: To indicate your intention to turn or change lanes.

Explanation: A turn signal, or blinker, is used to indicate your intention to turn or change lanes. It alerts other drivers of your intentions on the road, helping to prevent accidents.
Question 136: What is an intersection?
Answer: A place where two or more roads meet or cross each other.
Explanation: An intersection is a place where two or more roads meet or cross each other. Intersections can be controlled by traffic signals, signs, or be uncontrolled.
Question 137: What does a green traffic light indicate?
Answer: Go, if it is safe to do so.
Explanation: A green traffic light indicates that you can proceed, but only if the intersection or road ahead is clear. You must yield to any vehicle or pedestrian still in the intersection.
Question 138: What is a U-turn?
Answer: A 180-degree turn to go in the opposite direction.
Explanation: A U-turn is a driving maneuver that involves making a 180-degree turn to go in the opposite direction. U-turns are not allowed where they would interfere with traffic and are often restricted by local laws.
Question 139: What do you do if your car's accelerator sticks while you're driving?
Answer: Shift to neutral, apply the brakes, and safely pull off the road.
Explanation: If your car's accelerator sticks while you're driving, don't panic. Shift the car into neutral, apply the brakes, and steer the car to a safe spot off the road. Turn off the engine once you've stopped safely. Don't try to force the pedal up while driving.
Question 140: What does it mean to "yield" in traffic?
Answer: Letting other road users go first.
Explanation: To "yield" in traffic means to let other road users go first. A yield sign indicates that a driver must prepare to stop if necessary to let a driver on another approach proceed.
Question 141: What should you do if an oncoming vehicle has its high beams on?
Answer: Avoid looking directly into the oncoming headlights—look toward the right edge of your lane.
Explanation: If an oncoming vehicle has its high beams on, avoid looking directly into the oncoming headlights—instead, look toward the right edge of your lane. Watch the oncoming car out of the corner of your eye. Do not try to retaliate by switching to your high beams, which will only increase glare and limit visibility for both you and the oncoming vehicle.

Question 142: What is the main cause of tire blowouts?
Answer: Underinflation.
Explanation: Underinflation is the leading cause of tire blowouts. When a tire is underinflated, more of the tire's surface area touches the road, which increases friction and can cause the tire to overheat, leading to a blowout.
Question 143: What does a flashing red traffic light mean?
Answer: Stop and proceed when safe.
Explanation: A flashing red traffic light operates like a stop sign. Drivers should come to a complete stop, yield to oncoming traffic and pedestrians, and proceed when it is safe to do so.
Question 144: What should you do if you encounter a duststorm while driving?
Answer: Pull over to the side of the road, turn off your lights, and wait for the storm to pass.
Explanation: If you encounter a dust storm while driving, the best course of action is to pull over to the side of the road as far off the pavement as possible. Then, turn off your lights and wait for the storm to pass. Turning off your lights ensures that other drivers won't mistakenly follow you, thinking you're on the road.
Question 145: What is a roundabout in terms of road infrastructure?
Answer: A circular intersection where traffic flows counterclockwise around a central island.
Explanation: A roundabout is a type of circular intersection where traffic flows counterclockwise around a central island. Vehicles entering the roundabout must yield to traffic already in the circle.
Question 146: What does a solid white line indicate on the road?
Answer: You should stay within your lane and crossing it may be unsafe.
Explanation: A solid white line on the road usually marks the right edge of the roadway or separates lanes of traffic moving in the same direction. Crossing a solid white line may be unsafe and is discouraged.
Question 147: What should you do if your vehicle starts to skid?
Answer: Ease off the accelerator or brake, and steer in the direction of the skid.
Explanation: If your vehicle starts to skid, you should ease off the accelerator or brake. Then, steer in the direction that the rear of the vehicle is skidding. This action can help you regain control of the vehicle.
Question 148: What does a red traffic light indicate?
Answer: Stop.

Explanation: A red traffic light requires drivers to make a complete stop at the stop line, or if there is no stop line, before entering the intersection.
Question 149: What does an orange traffic cone usually signify on the road?
Answer: Caution, construction or temporary traffic control.
Explanation: Orange traffic cones are typically used to mark areas where drivers need to be cautious or to indicate construction zones. They can also signal temporary traffic control due to an accident or other obstruction.
Question 150: What is the three-second rule in driving?
Answer: A guideline for safe following distance.
Explanation: The three-second rule is a guideline drivers can use to establish a safe following distance from the vehicle ahead. After the vehicle ahead passes a certain point, such as a sign or a building, count "one thousand one, one thousand two, one thousand three." If you reach the same point before you finish counting, you are following too closely.
Question 151: What do you do when you approach a stop sign?
Answer: Come to a complete stop, yield to all other traffic and pedestrians, and proceed when it's safe.
Explanation: When you approach a stop sign, you must come to a complete stop at the stop line, or if there is no line, at the point nearest the intersecting roadway where the driver has a view of approaching traffic. Yield to all other traffic and pedestrians, and proceed when it's safe.
Question 152: What is a pedestrian crosswalk?
Answer: Designated area for pedestrians to cross the road.
Explanation: A pedestrian crosswalk is a designated area for pedestrians to cross the road. Vehicles must yield to pedestrians in or about to enter a crosswalk.
Question 153: What does a flashing yellow traffic light mean?
Answer: Proceed with caution.
Explanation: A flashing yellow traffic light requires drivers to slow down, proceed with caution, and be prepared to yield to oncoming traffic or pedestrians.
Question 154: What is a shoulder on a road?
Answer: An emergency stopping lane by the roadside.
Explanation: A shoulder is a reserved area by the verge of a road or motorway. It is designed for emergency stops and is also where emergency and recovery vehicles can operate.
Question 155: What do you do when you approach a yield sign?
Answer: Slow down, prepare to stop, and proceed only when it's

safe.
Explanation: When you approach a yield sign, you should slow down, prepare to stop, and yield the right-of-way to vehicles and pedestrians in the intersection or crosswalk. Proceed only when it's safe.
Question 156: What does a white rectangular sign indicate?
Answer: Regulatory or law information.
Explanation: White rectangular signs with black or red lettering or symbols are used to regulate traffic. They display regulations that drivers must obey such as speed limits, turn restrictions, or parking regulations.
Question 157: What is the purpose of rumble strips on the road?
Answer: To alert inattentive drivers of potential danger.
Explanation: Rumble strips are a road safety feature that causes a vibration and audible rumbling transmitted through the wheels into the vehicle interior. They are used to alert inattentive drivers of potential danger, such as approaching stop signs or the edges of the road.
Question 158: What is the purpose of a crosswalk?
Answer: To provide a designated area for pedestrians to cross the road.
Explanation: Crosswalks are designed to keep pedestrians together where they can be seen by motorists, and where they can cross most safely across the flow of vehicular traffic.
Question 159: What does a red and white triangular sign mean on the road?
Answer: Yield.
Explanation: A red and white triangular sign on the road is typically a "Yield" sign. Drivers must slow down and prepare to stop if necessary, to let any vehicles, bicyclists, or pedestrians pass before driving further.
Question 160: What should you do if you are involved in a minor car accident?
Answer: Move to a safe area (if you can), call the police, exchange information, document the accident, notify your insurer.
Explanation: If you're involved in a minor car accident, you should first move to a safe area if possible to avoid blocking traffic or risking additional collisions. Then, call the police, even if the accident is minor. Next, exchange information with the other driver(s) involved, including names, contact information, driver's license numbers, license plate numbers, and insurance information. Document the accident as best you can, taking pictures and making notes. Finally, notify your insurance company as soon as possible.

Question 161: What is a traffic island?
Answer: A raised area in the middle of a road, used to separate traffic in different directions or for pedestrians to cross.
Explanation: A traffic island is a solid or painted object in a road that channelizes traffic. It can be used to separate traffic moving in different directions, or to provide a safe space for pedestrians to stop before completing a crossing of a road.
Question 162: What happens when you get a DUI/DWI?
Answer: Legal consequences including fines, license suspension, possible jail time, and increased insurance rates.
Explanation: DUI/DWI (Driving Under the Influence/Driving While Intoxicated) offenses carry serious legal consequences. These may include large fines, suspension or revocation of your driver's license, mandatory alcohol education programs, possible jail or prison time, and increased car insurance rates. The specific consequences vary by location and whether it's a first or repeat offense.
Question 163: What does a blue traffic sign indicate?
Answer: Road user services, tourist information, and evacuation routes.
Explanation: Blue traffic signs often offer information to assist motorists. This can include road user services, such as food, gas, rest area indications, as well as tourist information. They can also be used to indicate evacuation routes.
Question 164: What is the purpose of the median strip on a highway?
Answer: To separate traffic moving in opposite directions.
Explanation: The median strip on a highway is designed to separate traffic moving in opposite directions. This helps to prevent head-on collisions and provides a safe zone for emergency vehicles.
Question 165: What does a dashed white line on the road mean?
Answer: You may change lanes if it is safe to do so.
Explanation: Dashed white lines on the road separate traffic lanes for vehicles traveling in the same direction. If the line between lanes is dashed, drivers may cross it when it's safe to change lanes.
Question 166: What is a "No U-turn" sign?
Answer: A sign that prohibits drivers from making a U-turn.
Explanation: A "No U-turn" sign is a traffic sign that prohibits drivers from making a U-turn. A U-turn is a vehicle maneuver that swaps the direction of travel to the opposite.
Question 167: What should you do if you see a "School Zone" sign?
Answer: Slow down, obey speed limits, and watch for children.

Explanation: A "School Zone" sign indicates you're nearing a zone with a nearby school where children might be present. You should slow down, obey the posted speed limits, and watch for children crossing the road or bicyclists.
Question 168: What does a "Slippery When Wet" sign mean?
Answer: The road may be particularly slippery when it's wet or raining.
Explanation: A "SlipperyWhen Wet" sign is a warning sign indicating that the roadway surface becomes particularly slick and may cause vehicles to skid or lose control when it is wet or raining. Drivers are advised to slow down and exercise caution when they see this sign, especially in wet weather.
Question 169: What does a "Do Not Enter" sign mean?
Answer: You are not allowed to enter the road or area ahead.
Explanation: A "Do Not Enter" sign is a regulatory sign that indicates a one-way street or restricted entry. Vehicles are prohibited from entering the roadway or area designated by this sign.
Question 170: What is the purpose of a roundabout in traffic?
Answer: To manage traffic intersections efficiently and safely.
Explanation: Roundabouts are designed to make intersections safer and more efficient for drivers, cyclists, and pedestrians. They reduce severe crashes, reduce delays, and improve traffic flow by encouraging continuous movement with less stop-and-go compared to signalized intersections.
Question 171: What does a "Yield" sign mean?
Answer: You must give way to the traffic on the road you are entering or crossing.
Explanation: A "Yield" sign is a regulatory sign that instructs drivers to slow down, defer to oncoming or intersecting traffic, stop when necessary, and proceed when it's safe to do so.
Question 172: What is the purpose of a bike lane on the road?
Answer: To provide a designated space for bicyclists.
Explanation: Bike lanes are sections of road designated for exclusive use by cyclists. They make the road safer for both cyclists and motorists by providing a separate space for bikes, reducing potential conflicts and collisions.
Question 173: What is a "Stop" sign?
Answer: A sign that instructs drivers to come to a complete stop.
Explanation: A "Stop" sign is a regulatory sign that instructs drivers to make a complete stop at the marked stop line. If no stop line is present, drivers should stop before entering the crosswalk or intersection.

Question 174: What is the purpose of a speed bump?
Answer: To slow down vehicles.
Explanation: Speed bumps are raised areas of a road designed to slow traffic or reduce through traffic. By forcing drivers to slow down to avoid an uncomfortable jolt, they improve safety for pedestrians and other road users.
Question 175: What does a "Road Work Ahead" sign mean?
Answer: There is construction or maintenance activity on or near the roadway ahead.
Explanation: A "Road Work Ahead" sign is a warning sign indicating that there is road work or construction activity occurring on or near the roadway ahead. Drivers should be prepared for unusual or potentially dangerous conditions, and should slow down and heed directions from flaggers and other workers.
Question 176: What is a "Detour" sign?
Answer: A sign that guides drivers to follow an alternative route.
Explanation: A "Detour" sign is a traffic sign that guides drivers to follow an alternative route, typically because the usual road is temporarily closed due to road work or because of an emergency.
Question 177: What is a pedestrian crossing?
Answer: A designated place for pedestrians to cross a road.
Explanation: A pedestrian crossing or crosswalk is a designated point on a road at which some means are employed to assist pedestrians wishing to cross safely. They are designed to keep pedestrians together where they can be seen by motorists, and where they can cross most safely across the flow of vehicular traffic.
Question 178: What does a flashing yellow traffic light mean?
Answer: Proceed with caution.
Explanation: A flashing yellow traffic light is a signal to drivers to slow down and proceed with caution. Drivers should be prepared to stop if necessary.
Question 179: What is the purpose of a traffic light?
Answer: To control the flow of traffic at intersections.
Explanation: Traffic lights, also known as traffic signals, are signaling devices positioned at road intersections, pedestrian crossings, and other locations to control the flow of traffic. They assign the right of way to road users in order to help prevent accidents.
Question 180: What does a flashing red traffic light mean?
Answer: Stop and proceed when safe.
Explanation: A flashing red traffic light operates like a stop sign.

Drivers must come to a complete stop and then proceed when it is safe to do so.
Question 181: What does a solid yellow traffic light mean?
Answer: The light is about to change to red.
Explanation: A solid yellow traffic light is a warning that the light is about to change to red.
Question 182: What does a solid green traffic light mean?
Answer: Go, if it is safe to do so.
Explanation: A solid green traffic light indicates that you may proceed through the intersection if it is safe to do so. You should still be cautious and watch for pedestrians and oncoming traffic.
Question 183: What does a green arrow signal mean at a traffic light?
Answer: You have the right-of-way to make the indicated turn.
Explanation: A green arrow signal at a traffic light indicates you have the right-of-way and may make the turn indicated by the arrow, as long as it is safe and clear to do so.
Question 184: What is a "Wrong Way" sign?
Answer: A sign indicating you are traveling in the wrong direction.
Explanation: A "Wrong Way" sign is a traffic sign used to alert motorists that they are traveling in the wrong direction on a roadway, and they need to turn around.
Question 185: What does a "One Way" sign mean?
Answer: Traffic is allowed to move in one direction only.
Explanation: A "One Way" sign is a traffic sign that indicates that traffic is allowed to move in one direction only. The sign is used to prevent accidents and improve traffic flow.
Question 186: What is a "Merge" sign?
Answer: A sign indicating that two lanes of traffic are about to become one.
Explanation: A "Merge" sign is a traffic sign used to notify drivers that two separate roadways will come together into one lane. Drivers in both lanes are equally responsible for merging safely.
Question 187: What is a "Lane Ends" sign?
Answer: A sign indicating that the lane you're in is about to end.
Explanation: A "Lane Ends" sign is a traffic sign that warns drivers that the lane they are currently traveling in is about to end, and they will need to merge into another lane.
Question 188: What is a "No Parking" sign?
Answer: A sign indicating that parking is not allowed.
Explanation: A "No Parking" sign is a traffic sign that indicates that vehicles are not allowed to park in that area, either during certain hours or at any time.

Question 189: What is a "No Standing" sign?
Answer: A sign indicating that you may not stop your vehicle except for loading or unloading passengers.
Explanation: A "No Standing" sign is a traffic sign that means you are only allowed to stop temporarily to load or unload passengers. It's not intended for parking or waiting.
Question 190: What is a "No Stopping" sign?
Answer: A sign indicating that stopping is not allowed.
Explanation: A "No Stopping" sign is a traffic sign that prohibits drivers from stopping their vehicles in the area indicated by the sign, whether it's to load or unload passengers or goods.
Question 191: What are road lines?
Answer: Markings that provide guidance and information about the road's alignment, the position of the vehicle and its maneuvering.
Explanation: Road lines or road markings are used to provide guidance and information to drivers and pedestrians. They can indicate the boundary of the road, provide navigational guidance, or enforce regulatory rules such as no overtaking zones.
Question 192: What is a double yellow line?
Answer: A road marking that separates traffic flowing in opposite directions, where passing is not allowed.
Explanation: Double yellow lines in the center of a roadway indicate that traffic is traveling in both directions, and passing (changing lanes to overtake another vehicle) is not allowed for vehicles traveling in either direction.
Question 193: What is a single yellow line?
Answer: A road marking that may indicate various restrictions depending on the local law.
Explanation: The meaning of a single yellow line can vary depending on the country or region. Generally, it indicates some form of parking or stopping restriction.
Question 194: What is a solid white line?
Answer: A road marking that separates lanes of traffic moving in the same direction, where changing lanes is discouraged.
Explanation: Solid white lines are used to mark the right edge of the road or to separate lanes of traffic moving in the same direction. Crossing a solid white line is generally discouraged unless necessary.
Question 195: What is a "Pedestrian Crossing" sign?
Answer: A sign indicating a designated pedestrian crossing point.
Explanation: A "Pedestrian Crossing" sign is used to alert drivers to locations where pedestrians might be crossing the road. Drivers should be prepared to stop to196. **Question 196:** What does a

"School Zone" sign mean?
Answer: A sign indicating an area near a school where special traffic laws apply.
Explanation: A "School Zone" sign is a traffic sign used to indicate an area where school children may be crossing the road or might be present. Speed limits are often reduced, and drivers are expected to be particularly cautious.
Question 197: What does a "Speed Limit" sign mean?
Answer: A sign indicating the maximum legal speed for a section of road.
Explanation: A "Speed Limit" sign is a traffic sign that indicates the maximum legal speed that vehicles may travel on that section of road. The limit is set for safety reasons and may vary depending on the type of road and its surroundings.
Question 198: What does a "Stop" sign mean?
Answer: A sign indicating that drivers must come to a complete stop.
Explanation: A "Stop" sign is a traffic sign that requires each driver to come to a complete stop before proceeding. They must yield to all other traffic and pedestrians before moving ahead.
Question 199: What does a "Yield" sign mean?
Answer: A sign indicating that drivers must prepare to stop if necessary to let other road users go first.
Explanation: A "Yield" sign is a traffic sign that requires drivers to slow down or stop if necessary to let other road users (vehicles, bicycles, pedestrians) go first. It is typically used where minor roads meet major roads.
Question 200: What does a "Do Not Enter" sign mean?
Answer: A sign indicating that a road or area is off limits to certain types of traffic.
Explanation: A "Do Not Enter" sign is a traffic sign that indicates a road or area is off limits to certain types of traffic, typically vehicles. It is often used to mark one-way streets or restricted-access roads.
Question 201: What is a "No U-Turn" sign?
Answer: A sign indicating that U-turns are prohibited.
Explanation: A "No U-Turn" sign is a traffic sign that prohibits drivers from making a U-turn, a 180-degree turn to reverse the direction of travel.
Question 202: What is a "No Left Turn" sign?
Answer: A sign indicating that left turns are prohibited.
Explanation: A "No Left Turn" sign is a traffic sign that prohibits

drivers from making a left turn at an intersection or onto another road.
Question 203: What is a "No Right Turn" sign?
Answer: A sign indicating that right turns are prohibited.
Explanation: A "No Right Turn" sign is a traffic sign that prohibits drivers from making a right turn at an intersection or onto another road.
Question 204: What is a "No Trucks" sign?
Answer: A sign indicating that trucks or commercial vehicles are prohibited.
Explanation: A "No Trucks" sign is a traffic sign that prohibits trucks or commercial vehicles from using a particular road or area, often because of weight limits or low clearance.
Question 205: What is a "Roundabout" sign?
Answer: A sign indicating the presence of a roundabout ahead.
Explanation: A "Roundabout" sign is a traffic sign that alerts drivers of an upcoming roundabout, a type of circular intersection where traffic flows continuously in one direction around a central island.
Question 206: What are "Bicycle Lane" signs?
Answer: Signs indicating a road lane designated for the exclusive or primary use of bicycles.
Explanation: "Bicycle Lane" signs are used to designate lanes on the road that are reserved for cyclists. These lanes are typically marked by signs and road markings and are designed to provide a safe space for cyclists on the road.
Question 207: What is a "Handicap Parking" sign?
Answer: A sign indicating parking spaces reserved for individuals with disabilities.
Explanation: A "Handicap Parking" sign, also known as a disabled parking sign, is used to designate parking spaces that are reserved for individuals with disabilities. These spaces are typically located close to building entrances for easier access.
Question 208: What is a "Fire Lane" sign?
Answer: A sign indicating a road or zone that is restricted for emergency vehicles.
Explanation: A "Fire Lane" sign designates an area that is to be kept clear for fire trucks and other emergency vehicles. Parking or stopping in these areas is typically prohibited.
Question 209: What is a "Slippery When Wet" sign?
Answer: A sign warning drivers that the road surface may be slippery when it's wet or raining.
Explanation: A "Slippery When Wet" sign is a traffic sign used to

alert drivers that the road conditions may be slippery when wet, advising them to take extra caution while driving.

Question 210: What is a "Falling Rocks" sign?

Answer: A sign warning of the potential for falling rocks from steep cliffs or mountainsides.

Explanation: A "Falling Rocks" sign is used in areas where the risk of rocks or debris falling onto the road is higher, usually in mountainous or hilly areas. It's a warning to drivers to be vigilant.

Question 211: What is a "Sharp Curve" sign?

Answer: A sign warning drivers of a sharp curve ahead in the road.

Explanation: A "Sharp Curve" sign is used to warn drivers that a sharp or unexpected curve is coming up. This sign is typically used when the curve is so sharp that it requires drivers to reduce their speed to navigate it safely.

Question 212: What is a "Steep Hill" sign?

Answer: A sign indicating a steep incline or decline ahead on the road.

Explanation: A "Steep Hill" sign is used to warn drivers that a steep incline or decline is coming up on the road. This sign is typically used in hilly or mountainous areas.

Question 213: What is a "School Bus Stop Ahead" sign?

Answer: A sign warning drivers that they are approaching a designated school bus stop.

Explanation: A "School Bus Stop Ahead" sign is used to alert drivers that they are approaching an area where school buses stop to pick up or drop off students. Drivers should be prepared to stop and yield to children crossing the road.

Question 214: What is a "Railroad Crossing" sign?

Answer: A sign warning drivers that they are approaching a railroad crossing.

Explanation: A "Railroad Crossing" sign is used to alert drivers that they are approaching a location where a road crosses a railway line. Drivers should be prepared to stop if a train is approaching.

Question 215: What is an "Animal Crossing" sign?

Answer: A sign indicating a location where wild animals frequently cross the road.

Explanation: An "Animal Crossing" sign is used to alert drivers to areas where wild animals frequently cross the road. It's a warning to drivers to be vigilant and prepared to stop to avoid collisions with animals.

Question 216: What is a "Bump" or "Dip" sign?

Answer: A sign warning drivers about a sudden change in road

surface.
Explanation: A "Bump" or "Dip" sign is used to alert drivers to a sudden change in the road surface. A "bump" sign warns of a raised section of road, while a "dip" sign warns of a lowered section.
Question 217: What is a "Road Work Ahead" sign?
Answer: A sign warning drivers of upcoming roadwork or construction.
Explanation: A "Road Work Ahead" sign is used to alert drivers to upcoming road work or construction. It's a warning to drivers to slow down, watch for workers and machinery, and be prepared for changes in the road surface or detours.
Question 218: What is a "Detour" sign?
Answer: A sign indicating an alternative route for drivers to take due to road work or a road closure.
Explanation: A "Detour" sign is used to guide drivers along an alternative route when the normal road is closed or obstructed, usually due to road work or an accident.
Question 219: What is a "Flagger Ahead" sign?
Answer: A sign warning drivers that there is a flagger (a person providing traffic control) ahead.
Explanation: A "Flagger Ahead" sign is used in road work zones to alert drivers that a person (a flagger) is ahead to direct traffic around the work zone. Drivers should be prepared to obey the flagger's instructions.
Question 220: What is a "Speed Bump" sign?
Answer: A sign warning drivers about a speed bump ahead.
Explanation: A "Speed Bump" sign is used to alert drivers to an upcoming speed bump, a raised portion of road designed to slow traffic. Drivers should be prepared to slow down to navigate the speed bump safely.
Question 221: What is an "End of Road Work" sign?
Answer: A sign indicating the end of a road work or construction zone.
Explanation: An "End of Road Work" sign is used to indicate to drivers that they have passed through the road work or construction zone and normal road conditions resume.
Question 222: What is a "No Parking" sign?
Answer: A sign indicating that parking is not allowed in a specific area.
Explanation: A "No Parking" sign is a regulatory sign used to indicate areas where parking is prohibited.

Question 223: What is a "No U-Turn" sign?
Answer: A sign indicating that U-turns are not allowed.
Explanation: A "No U-Turn" sign is a regulatory sign used to prohibit drivers from making a U-turn, a maneuver to change direction on the road.
Question 224: What is a "No Passing Zone" sign?
Answer: A sign indicating that passing other vehicles is not allowed in a specific area.
Explanation: A "No Passing Zone" sign is a regulatory sign used to indicate areas where passing (overtaking another vehicle traveling in the same direction) is prohibited.
Question 225: What is a "Stop" sign?
Answer: A sign instructing drivers to come to a complete stop before proceeding.
Explanation: A "Stop" sign is a regulatory sign used to instruct drivers to come to a complete stop at an intersection or road junction, look for other vehicles or pedestrians, and then proceed when it is safe to do so.
Question 226: What is a "Yield" sign?
Answer: A sign instructing drivers to slow down or stop if necessary and yield the right-of-way to other vehicles or pedestrians.
Explanation: A "Yield" sign is a regulatory sign used to instruct drivers to slow down or stop if necessary and yield the right-of-way to other vehicles or pedestrians.
Question 227: What is a "Do Not Enter" sign?
Answer: A sign indicating that a road or area is off-limits to certain types of traffic.
Explanation: A "Do Not Enter" sign is a regulatory sign used to indicate roads or areas where certain types of traffic, usually vehicular, are prohibited.
Question 228: What is a "One Way" sign?
Answer: A sign indicating that traffic flows in only one direction on a particular road.
Explanation: A "One Way" sign is a regulatory sign used to indicate that traffic flows in only one direction on a particular road.
Question 229: What is a "Truck Route" sign?
Answer: A sign indicating a route designed for truck traffic.
Explanation: A "Truck Route" sign is used to direct trucks or commercial vehicles along roads that are designed to handle their size and weight.
Question 230: What is a "Bicycle Lane" sign?
Answer: A sign indicating a lane specifically designated for bicycle

use.
Explanation: A "Bicycle Lane" sign is used to indicate a lane specifically designated for the use of bicycles. These lanes are typically marked with distinctive road markings.
Question 231: What is a "Pedestrian Crossing" sign?
Answer: A sign indicating a designated pedestrian crossing area.
Explanation: A "Pedestrian Crossing" sign is used to indicate a designated area where pedestrians may cross a road. Drivers are typically required to yield to pedestrians in these areas.
Question 232: What is a "Handicap Parking" sign?
Answer: A sign indicating a parking space reserved for individuals with disabilities.
Explanation: A "Handicap Parking" sign is used to designate parking spaces that are reserved for individuals with disabilities. These spaces are typically located near building entrances and are often larger to accommodate vehicles with wheelchair lifts or ramps.
Question 233: What is a "Motorcycle Parking" sign?
Answer: A sign indicating a parking space reserved for motorcycles.
Explanation: A "Motorcycle Parking" sign is used to designate parking spaces that are reserved for motorcycles.
Question 234: What is a "Bus Stop" sign?
Answer: A sign indicating a designated bus stop location.
Explanation: A "Bus Stop" sign is used to designate areas where buses stop to pick up and drop off passengers.
Question 235: What is a "Taxi Stand" sign?
Answer: A sign indicating a designated location for taxis to wait for passengers.
Explanation: A "Taxi Stand" sign is used to designate areas where taxis are allowed to wait for passengers. Typically, these are located at airports, train stations, hotels, and other high-traffic areas.
Question 236: What is a "Hospital" sign?
Answer: A sign indicating the location of a hospital.
Explanation: A "Hospital" sign is used to direct people to the nearest medical facility. The sign typically includes a symbol of a bed or a white "H" on a blue background.
Question 237: What is a "Restaurant" sign?
Answer: A sign indicating the location of a restaurant.
Explanation: A "Restaurant" sign is used to direct people to a place where they can buy and eat meals. The sign could include the

name of the restaurant or a general symbol representing a restaurant.
Question 238: What is a "Hotel" sign?
Answer: A sign indicating the location of a hotel.
Explanation: A "Hotel" sign is used to direct people to a place where they can rent a room to stay overnight. The sign could include the name of the hotel or a general symbol representing a hotel.
Question 239: What is a "Gas Station" sign?
Answer: A sign indicating the location of a gas station.
Explanation: A "Gas Station" sign is used to direct people to a place where they can buy fuel for their vehicles. The sign could include the name of the gas station or a general symbol representing a gas station.
Question 240: What is a "Parking" sign?
Answer: A sign indicating the location of a parking area.
Explanation: A "Parking" sign is used to direct drivers to a place where they can park their vehicles. These signs often indicate whether parking is free or paid, and whether there are any restrictions.
Question 241: What is a "Rest Area" sign?
Answer: A sign indicating the location of a rest area along a highway.
Explanation: A "Rest Area" sign is used to direct drivers to a place where they can stop to rest, use restroom facilities, and sometimes purchase food and fuel. These are typically found along highways and interstates.
Question 242: What is a "Speed Limit" sign?
Answer: A sign indicating the maximum speed at which drivers can legally travel on a particular road.
Explanation: A "Speed Limit" sign is used to inform drivers of the maximum speed that is legally allowed on the road. The limit is often set based on the road's conditions and surrounding environment to ensure safety.
Question 243: What is a "Merge" sign?
Answer: A sign warning drivers to prepare to merge with other traffic.
Explanation: A "Merge" sign is used to warn drivers that they will need to merge with other traffic, usually because two lanes are becoming one, or a ramp is joining the main road.
Question 244: What is a "Lane Ends" sign?
Answer: A sign warning drivers that their lane is ending.
Explanation: A "Lane Ends" sign is used to warn drivers that their

lane is ending and they will need to merge with traffic in another lane.
Question 245: What is a "Roundabout" sign?
Answer: A sign warning drivers that they are approaching a roundabout.
Explanation: A "Roundabout" sign is used to warn drivers that they are approaching a roundabout, a type of circular intersection where traffic flows continuously in one direction around a central island.
Question 246: What is a "Yield Ahead" sign?
Answer: A sign warning drivers that they are approaching a yield sign.
Explanation: A "Yield Ahead" sign is used to warn drivers that they are approaching a yield sign, where they will need to slow or stop to give right of way to other traffic.
Question 247: What is a "Stop Ahead" sign?
Answer: A sign warning drivers that they are approaching a stop sign.
Explanation: A "Stop Ahead" sign is used to warn drivers that they are approaching a stop sign, where they will need to come to a complete stop and give right of way to other traffic.
Question 248: What is a "Signal Ahead" sign?
Answer: A sign warning drivers that they are approaching a traffic signal.
Explanation: A "Signal Ahead" sign is used to warn drivers that they are approaching a traffic signal, where they will need to follow the249. **Question 249:** What is a "School Zone" sign?
Answer: A sign indicating that drivers are entering an area near a school where special traffic rules apply.
Explanation: A "School Zone" sign is used to alert drivers to slow down and be extra cautious as children may be crossing the road or behaving unpredictably near a school.
Question 250: What is a "Pedestrian Crossing" sign?
Answer: A sign indicating a designated location where pedestrians are allowed to cross the road.
Explanation: A "Pedestrian Crossing" sign is used to alert drivers to locations where pedestrians may be crossing the road, and to remind drivers to yield to pedestrians.
Question 251: What is a "Bicycle Lane" sign?
Answer: A sign indicating a lane specifically designated for bicycle traffic.
Explanation: A "Bicycle Lane" sign is used to designate lanes

specifically for bicycle use. These lanes are typically separated from motor vehicle traffic by a solid or dashed line.
Question 252: What is a "No Parking" sign?
Answer: A sign indicating areas where parking is prohibited.
Explanation: A "No Parking" sign is used to alert drivers to areas where parking is not allowed, often to ensure the free flow of traffic or pedestrian safety.
Question 253: What is a "No U-Turn" sign?
Answer: A sign indicating that U-turns are prohibited.
Explanation: A "No U-Turn" sign is used to prevent drivers from making a U-turn, a maneuver to change direction of travel on a road. U-turns are prohibited in certain areas to ensure safe traffic flow.
Question 254: What is a "No Right Turn" sign?
Answer: A sign indicating that right turns are prohibited.
Explanation: A "No Right Turn" sign is used to prevent drivers from making a right turn, often to ensure the safety and smooth flow of traffic at busy or complex intersections.
Question 255: What is a "No Left Turn" sign?
Answer: A sign indicating that left turns are prohibited.
Explanation: A "No Left Turn" sign is used to prevent drivers from making a left turn, often to ensure the safety and smooth flow of traffic at busy or complex intersections.
Question 256: What is a "One Way" sign?
Answer: A sign indicating that traffic flows in one direction only.
Explanation: A "One Way" sign is used to designate roads where vehicles are allowed to travel in one direction only. This is often done to increase traffic efficiency and safety.
Question 257: What is a "Dead End" sign?
Answer: A sign indicating that the road does not continue beyond a certain point.
Explanation: A "Dead End" sign is used to alert drivers that the road does not continue beyond a certain point, meaning they will need to turn around or exit via the same route they entered.
Question 258: What is a "Do Not Enter" sign?
Answer: A sign indicating that vehicles are not allowed to enter the roadway or area beyond the sign.
Explanation: A "Do Not Enter" sign is used to prevent vehicles from entering a certain area or roadway. This is often used on one-way streets, restricted areas, or at the exits of certain facilities.
Question 259: What is a "Construction Ahead" sign?
Answer: A sign indicating that there is construction activity ahead on the road.

Explanation: A "Construction Ahead" sign is used to warn drivers of upcoming construction work. These signs often include additional information about the nature of the work, any potential hazards, and how drivers should navigate the work zone.
Question 260: What is a "Slippery When Wet" sign?
Answer: A sign warning drivers that the road surface may be slippery when wet.
Explanation: A "Slippery When Wet" sign is used to warn drivers that the road surface may become slippery during wet weather. This often applies to roads that are made of materials or have a surface condition that may become slick in rain, snow, or ice.
Question 261: What is a "Narrow Bridge" sign?
Answer: A sign warning drivers that the bridge ahead is narrower than the approach road.
Explanation: A "Narrow Bridge" sign is used to warn drivers that they are approaching a bridge which may be narrower than the road leading up to it. This is to alert drivers to adjust their speed and position to safely navigate the bridge.
Question 262: What is a "Cattle Crossing" sign?
Answer: A sign warning drivers that they are in an area where cattle may cross the road.
Explanation: A "Cattle Crossing" sign is used in rural areas to warn drivers that they may encounter cattle crossing the road, urging them to slow down and drive carefully.
Question 263: What is a "Deer Crossing" sign?
Answer: A sign warning drivers that they are in an area where deer may cross the road.
Explanation: A "Deer Crossing" sign is used to warn drivers that they are traveling in an area where deer are likely to cross the road, particularly at dawn and dusk, prompting them to slow down and be vigilant.
Question 264: What is a "Moose Crossing" sign?
Answer: A sign warning drivers that they are in an area where moose may cross the road.
Explanation: A "Moose Crossing" sign is used in areas where moose are common, warning drivers that they may encounter moose crossing the road, especially at dawn and dusk, and advising them to slow down and be vigilant.
Question 265: What is a "Bear Crossing" sign?
Answer: A sign warning drivers that they are in an area where bears may cross the road.
Explanation: A "Bear Crossing" sign is used in certain regions to warn drivers that they may encounter bears crossing the road,

particularly in wooded areas or near rivers, urging them to slow down and be vigilant.

Question 266: What is a "School Bus Stop Ahead" sign?

Answer: A sign warning drivers that they are approaching a designated school bus stop.

Explanation: A "School Bus Stop Ahead" sign is used to warn drivers that they are approaching a location where a school bus stops to pick up or drop off students, prompting drivers to slow down and prepare to stop if needed.

Question 267: What is a "Railroad Crossing" sign?

Answer: A sign warning drivers that they are approaching a railway crossing.

Explanation: A "Railroad Crossing" sign is used to warn drivers that they are approaching a location where a railway intersects the road, urging them to slow down, look both ways, and prepare to stop if a train is coming.

Question 268: What is a "Road Work Ahead" sign?

Answer: A sign warning drivers that they are approaching a work zone on the road.

Explanation: A "Road Work Ahead" sign is used to warn drivers that there is road construction or maintenance work ahead, prompting them to slow down, be cautious, and be prepared for changes in the roadway.

Question 269: What is a "Detour" sign?

Answer: A sign indicating that drivers must follow a different route due to a road closure or obstruction.

Explanation: A "Detour" sign is used to direct drivers to an alternate route when the usual path is closed or obstructed, often providing directions or a map to guide drivers around the closure.

Question 270: What is a "Slow Moving Vehicle" sign?

Answer: A sign used on vehicles that travel at slower speeds to warn other drivers.

Explanation: A "Slow Moving Vehicle" sign is often a reflective orange triangle used on vehicles like farm equipment, horse-drawn carriages, or construction equipment that travel at slower speeds, warning other drivers to slow down and pass with caution.

Question 271: What is a "Weight Limit" sign?

Answer: A sign indicating the maximum weight that a vehicle or combination of vehicles may weigh to use a certain road, bridge, or tunnel.

Explanation: A "Weight Limit" sign is used to prevent heavy vehicles from causing damage to roads, bridges, or tunnels that

cannot support heavy loads. The weight is typically expressed in tons.
Question 272: What is a "Height Limit" sign?
Answer: A sign indicating the maximum height of vehicles that can safely pass under a bridge, overpass, or other structure.
Explanation: A "Height Limit" sign is used to prevent tall vehicles from colliding with low-clearance structures. The height is typically listed in feet and possibly in meters.
Question 273: What is a "Width Limit" sign?
Answer: A sign indicating the maximumwidth of vehicles that can safely travel through a narrow passage, such as a gate or tunnel.
Explanation: A "Width Limit" sign is used to prevent wide vehicles from attempting to pass through narrow areas where they might get stuck or cause damage. The width is typically listed in feet and possibly in meters.
Question 274: What is a "No U-Turn" sign?
Answer: A sign that prohibits drivers from making a U-turn.
Explanation: A "No U-Turn" sign is used to prevent drivers from making a U-turn at locations where it is unsafe or disruptive to other traffic.
Question 275: What is a "No Parking" sign?
Answer: A sign that prohibits parking in a specific area.
Explanation: A "No Parking" sign is used to prevent vehicles from parking in certain areas, such as near fire hydrants, in front of driveways, or in areas where parking would obstruct traffic.
Question 276: What is a "No Standing" sign?
Answer: A sign that prohibits drivers from stopping their vehicle, except for the purpose of quickly picking up or dropping off passengers.
Explanation: A "No Standing" sign is used to prevent vehicles from idling or standing in certain areas, even if the driver remains in the vehicle, unless it's for the quick pick-up or drop-off of passengers.
Question 277: What is a "No Stopping" sign?
Answer: A sign that prohibits drivers from stopping their vehicle for any reason.
Explanation: A "No Stopping" sign is used to prevent vehicles from stopping in certain areas, even momentarily. Unlike "No Standing" signs, stopping is not permitted even for the quick pick-up or drop-off of passengers.
Question 278: What is a "Handicapped Parking" sign?
Answer: A sign designating parking spaces specifically for individuals with disabilities.

Explanation: A "Handicapped Parking" sign is used to reserve parking spaces for individuals with disabilities. These spaces are usually located close to building entrances and are wider than standard spaces to accommodate wheelchairs and other mobility devices.
Question 279: What is a "Hospital" sign?
Answer: A sign indicating the direction to a hospital.
Explanation: A "Hospital" sign is used to guide drivers to the nearest hospital. It is usually marked with a white "H" on a blue background.
Question 280: What is a "Bicycle Lane" sign?
Answer: A sign indicating a lane specifically designated for bicycles.
Explanation: A "Bicycle Lane" sign is used to designate a portion of the roadway for the exclusive use of bicycles. These lanes are usually marked with bike symbols and/or signs and are typically located on the right side of the road.
Question 281: What is a "Pedestrian Crossing" sign?
Answer: A sign warning drivers to be attentive for pedestrians crossing the road.
Explanation: A "Pedestrian Crossing" sign is used to alert drivers to locations where pedestrians may be crossing the road, such as a crosswalk or a school zone.
Question 282: What is a "School Zone" sign?
Answer: A sign indicating an area near a school where traffic laws are strictly enforced.
Explanation: A "School Zone" sign is used to warn drivers that they are entering an area near a school where children may be present, and speed limits are typically reduced.
Question 283: What is a "Slippery When Wet" sign?
Answer: A sign warning drivers that the road may become slippery in wet conditions.
Explanation: A "Slippery When Wet" sign is used to warn drivers that the road surface may become slippery when it is wet or raining, urging them to reduce speed and drive cautiously.
Question 284: What is a "Sharp Curve Ahead" sign?
Answer: A sign warning drivers that a sharp curve is coming up on the road.
Explanation: A "Sharp Curve Ahead" sign is used to warn drivers that they will need to reduce speed and use caution as they approach a sharp curve in the roadway.
Question 285: What is a "Two-Way Traffic" sign?
Answer: A sign indicating that traffic flows in both directions on

the road.
Explanation: A "Two-Way Traffic" sign is used to warn drivers that they are entering a section of road where traffic flows in both directions, usually after a one-way street or divided highway.
Question 286: What is a "Yield" sign?
Answer: A sign indicating that drivers must prepare to stop if necessary to let other drivers on the road proceed.
Explanation: A "Yield" sign is used to indicate that drivers should slow down or stop if necessary to let other road users go first, especially when merging onto another roadway.
Question 287: What is a "Stop" sign?
Answer: A sign indicating that drivers must come to a complete stop before proceeding.
Explanation: A "Stop" sign is used to indicate that drivers must come to a complete stop at an intersection and then proceed only when it is safe and legal to do so.
Question 288: What is a "Do Not Enter" sign?
Answer: A sign indicating that vehicles are prohibited from entering a particular roadway or area.
Explanation: A "Do Not Enter" sign is used to indicate that vehicles are not allowed to enter the indicated direction of a street or highway, typically used at one-way street exits or highway off-ramps.
Question 289: What is a "Wrong Way" sign?
Answer: A sign indicating that a vehicle is traveling in the wrong direction on a one-way street or highway ramp.
Explanation: A "Wrong Way" sign is used to indicate that a driver has entered a one-way street, ramp, or lane traveling in the wrong direction.
Question 290: What is a "No Trucks" sign?
Answer: A sign indicating that trucks are prohibited from using a certain roadway.
Explanation: A "No Trucks" sign is used to indicate that trucks or commercial vehicles are not allowed on certain roads, usually due to low clearance bridges, narrow roads, or residential zoning.
Question 291: What is a "One Way" sign?
Answer: A sign indicating that traffic flows in only one direction.
Explanation: A "One Way" sign is used to indicate that traffic on a particular street or lane flows only in the direction indicated by the arrow on the sign.
Question 292: What is a "Speed Limit" sign?
Answer: A sign indicating the maximum legal speed that vehicles can travel on a particular roadway.

Explanation: A "Speed Limit" sign is used to indicate the maximum legal speed for a section of road. Speed limits are set based on the type of road, its location, and safety considerations.
Question 293: What is a "Merge" sign?
Answer: A sign warning drivers that two lanes of traffic are about to become one.
Explanation: A "Merge" sign is used to warn drivers that they will need to either move into another lane of traffic or allow traffic from another lane to merge into their lane.
Question 294: What is a "Lane Ends" sign?
Answer: A sign warning drivers that their lane is about to end, and they will need to merge with traffic in another lane.
Explanation: A "Lane Ends" sign is used to warn drivers that their current lane will not continue, requiring them to merge safely into another lane.
Question 295: What is a "Roundabout" sign?
Answer: A sign indicating that there is a circular intersection or roundabout ahead.
Explanation: A "Roundabout" sign is used to warn drivers that they are approaching a roundabout, which is a type of circular intersection where traffic flows in one direction around a central island.
Question 296: What is a "Traffic Signal Ahead" sign?
Answer: A sign warning drivers that they are approaching an intersection controlled by a traffic signal.
Explanation: A "Traffic Signal Ahead" sign is used to warn drivers that they are approaching a traffic signal (such as a stoplight), particularly where the signal might not be clearly visible from a distance.
Question 297: What is a "Divided Highway Begins" sign?
Answer: A sign indicating that the road ahead is split into separate lanes for opposing traffic by a median or barrier.
Explanation: A "Divided Highway Begins" sign is used to warn drivers that they are approaching a point where the road splits into separate lanes for traffic traveling in opposite directions, separated by a median or barrier.
Question 298: What is a "Divided Highway Ends" sign?
Answer: A sign indicating that the divided highway is about to end, and the road will no longer be split into separate lanes for opposing traffic.
Explanation: A "Divided Highway Ends" sign is used to warn drivers that the divided section of the highway is about to end, and

they will soon be on a road where traffic flows in both directions on the same roadway.
Question299: What is a "Pedestrian Crossing" sign?
Answer: A sign indicating a designated crossing point for pedestrians.
Explanation: A "Pedestrian Crossing" sign is used to alert drivers to areas where they may encounter pedestrians crossing the road. This sign is often used near schools, parks, and populated areas.
Question 300: What is a "School Zone" sign?
Answer: A sign indicating a zone near a school where speed limits are reduced during school hours.
Explanation: A "School Zone" sign is used to warn drivers they are entering an area near a school where speed limits are often reduced during school hours to ensure the safety of students.
Question 301: What is a "Bicycle Crossing" sign?
Answer: A sign indicating a crossing point for bicycles.
Explanation: A "Bicycle Crossing" sign is used to alert drivers to areas where they may encounter bicyclists crossing the road. This sign is often used near parks, trails, and other areas frequented by bicyclists.
Question 302: What is a "Slippery When Wet" sign?
Answer: A sign indicating that the road surface might be especially slippery and dangerous when it's wet or raining.
Explanation: A "Slippery When Wet" sign is used to warn drivers that a section of road can become particularly slick and hazardous in wet conditions, encouraging them to reduce speed and drive with caution.
Question 303: What is a "Deer Crossing" sign?
Answer: A sign indicating an area where deer frequently cross the road.
Explanation: A "Deer Crossing" sign is used to alert drivers to areas where deer often cross the road, particularly in rural or wooded areas, to reduce the risk of vehicle-deer collisions.
Question 304: What is a "Road Work Ahead" sign?
Answer: A sign indicating upcoming road construction or maintenance activity.
Explanation: A "Road Work Ahead" sign is used to warn drivers that they are approaching a work zone where road construction or maintenance is taking place, encouraging them to reduce speed and be aware of workers and equipment.
Question 305: What is a "No U-Turn" sign?
Answer: A sign indicating that U-turns are prohibited.
Explanation: A "No U-Turn" sign is used to indicate that it is illegal

to make a U-turn at a certain location, typically because it would be unsafe or disrupt traffic flow.
Question 306: What is a "No Parking" sign?
Answer: A sign indicating that parking is not allowed in a certain area.
Explanation: A "No Parking" sign is used to indicate areas where vehicles may not park, either at certain times or at all, often to ensure clear visibility, access, or traffic flow.
Question 307: What is a "No Passing Zone" sign?
Answer: A sign indicating a stretch of road where it is unsafe and illegal to pass other vehicles.
Explanation: A "No Passing Zone" sign is used to mark areas where it is not safe to pass other vehicles due to limited visibility of oncoming traffic, such as curves or hills.
Question 308: What is a "Truck Route" sign?
Answer: A sign indicating a route designated for truck traffic.
Explanation: A "Truck Route" sign is used to guide trucks or commercial vehicles along routes that can accommodate their size and weight, often avoiding residential areas or roads with low bridges or other restrictions.
Question 309: What is a "Hospital" sign?
Answer: A sign indicating the direction to a nearby hospital.
Explanation: A "Hospital" sign is used to guide drivers to the nearest hospital, often essential in emergencies. The sign typically features a white "H" on a blue background.
Question 310: What is a "Fire Station" sign?
Answer: A sign indicating the location of a fire station.
Explanation: A "Fire Station" sign is used to mark the location of a fire station. Drivers should be aware that fire vehicles may enter the road without warning.
Question 311: What is a "Railroad Crossing" sign?
Answer: A sign indicating a point where a railway line intersects a road at the same level.
Explanation: A "Railroad Crossing" sign is used to warn drivers that they're approaching a point where a railroad track crosses the roadway at grade level, requiring them to stop when a train is approaching.
Question 313: What is a "Detour" sign?
Answer: A sign indicating a temporary route for traffic due to road work or closure.
Explanation: A "Detour" sign is used to direct traffic along a different route than usual due to road construction, an accident, or other temporary road closure.

Question 314: What is a "Weight Limit" sign?
Answer: A sign indicating the maximum weight a vehicle can be to travel on a certain road or bridge.
Explanation: A "Weight Limit" sign is used to protect roadways and bridges from damage caused by vehicles that are too heavy. It is especially important for commercial vehicles to obey these signs.
Question 315: What is a "Flashing Signal" sign?
Answer: A sign indicating an intersection or crossing point where a flashing light signal is used.
Explanation: A "Flashing Signal" sign is used to warn drivers of an upcoming intersection or crossing point that is controlled by a flashing light signal, which typically requires drivers to stop or proceed with caution.
Question 316: What is a "Steep Grade" sign?
Answer: A sign indicating a steep slope in the road ahead.
Explanation: A "Steep Grade" sign is used to warn drivers of a steep incline or decline in the road ahead, which may require the use of lower gears or increased caution, particularly for large or heavy vehicles.
Question 317: What is a "Low Clearance" sign?
Answer: A sign indicating a bridge or structure with a low height limit.
Explanation: A "Low Clearance" sign is used to warn drivers of a bridge, overpass, or other structure that has a low height limit. It's important for drivers of tall vehicles to heed these signs to avoid collisions.
Question 318: What is a "Sharp Curve" sign?
Answer: A sign indicating a sharp turn in the road ahead.
Explanation: A "Sharp Curve" sign is used to warn drivers of a sharp turn in the road ahead, requiring them to slow down and use caution.
Question 319: What is a "Narrow Bridge" sign?
Answer: A sign indicating a bridge that is narrower than the approach road.
Explanation: A "Narrow Bridge" sign is used to warn drivers that they are approaching a bridge that may be narrower than the road leading up to it, requiring additional caution and sometimes yielding to oncoming traffic.
Question 320: What is a "Falling Rocks" sign?
Answer: A sign indicating a potential for rocks or debris to fall onto the roadway.
Explanation: A "Falling Rocks" sign is used to warn drivers that

they are entering an area where rocks or other debris may fall onto the roadway, often due to nearby cliffs or steep slopes.
Question 321: What is a "Two-Way Traffic" sign?
Answer: A sign indicating that traffic flows in both directions on the road.
Explanation: A "Two-Way Traffic" sign is used to warn drivers that they are leaving a one-way roadway and entering a road with two-way traffic.
Question 322: What is a "Pedestrians Only" sign?
Answer: A sign indicating a zone or path that is only for pedestrian use.
Explanation: A "Pedestrians Only" sign is used to indicate areas where vehicle traffic is prohibited, such as sidewalks or pedestrian plazas.
Question 323: What is a "Bicycles Only" sign?
Answer: A sign indicating a lane or path that is only for bicycle use.
Explanation: A "Bicycles Only" sign is used to indicate lanes or paths where vehicle traffic is prohibited, often in parks or on certain city streets.
Question 324: What is a "No Bicycles" sign?
Answer: A sign indicating that bicycles are not allowed.
Explanation: A "No Bicycles" sign is used to indicate areas where bicycles are prohibited, such as certain sidewalks, pedestrian plazas, or roads.
Question 325: What is a "No Pedestrians" sign?
Answer: A sign indicating that pedestrians are not allowed.
Explanation: A "No Pedestrians" sign is used to indicate areas where pedestrian traffic is prohibited, often for safety reasons, such as highways or certain high-traffic streets.
Question 326: What is a "Crosswalk" sign?
Answer: A sign indicating a designated crossing point for pedestrians.
Explanation: A "Crosswalk" sign is used to indicate areas where pedestrians are allowed to cross the road. Drivers are typically required to yield to327. **Question 327:** What is a "Roundabout" sign?
Answer: A sign indicating a circular intersection where traffic flows in one direction around a central island.
Explanation: A "Roundabout" sign is used to warn drivers they are approaching a roundabout, a type of circular intersection where traffic flows counterclockwise (in countries where driving is on the

right) or clockwise (in countries where driving is on the left) around a central island.
Question 328: What is a "Yield" sign?
Answer: A sign indicating drivers must prepare to stop if necessary to let a driver on another approach proceed.
Explanation: A "Yield" sign is typically triangular and red with a white interior, and it is used to indicate that drivers must give way to other traffic. Drivers encountering a yield sign must slow down or stop if necessary to let traffic on the intersecting road pass before they proceed.
Question 329: What is a "Stop" sign?
Answer: A sign indicating drivers must stop completely before proceeding.
Explanation: A "Stop" sign is an octagonal traffic sign that instructs drivers to make a complete stop at the marked stop line. After stopping, the driver should only proceed when it is safe to do so.
Question 330: What is a "No Turn on Red" sign?
Answer: A sign indicating that turning on a red signal is prohibited.
Explanation: In many places, it is generally allowed to make a right turn at a red light after a complete stop (or a left turn from a one-way street to another one-way street). A "No Turn on Red" sign prohibits this action.
Question 331: What is a "Do Not Enter" sign?
Answer: A sign indicating that entry into a certain area or road is prohibited.
Explanation: A "Do Not Enter" sign is typically used to mark one-way roads or ramps, indicating that a driver should not enter the road or area in the direction they are heading.
Question 332: What is a "One Way" sign?
Answer: A sign indicating that traffic flows in only one direction.
Explanation: A "One Way" sign is used on one-way streets and ramps, instructing drivers to only proceed in the direction indicated by the arrow on the sign.
Question 333: What is a "Bus Stop" sign?
Answer: A sign indicating a designated stop for buses.
Explanation: A "Bus Stop" sign is used to mark the location where buses stop to pick up and drop off passengers. These signs often include information about the bus routes that stop there.
Question 334: What is a "Railroad Crossing" sign?
Answer: A sign indicating the presence of a railroad crossing ahead.

Explanation: A "Railroad Crossing" sign is used to warn drivers that they are approaching a location where a railway intersects with the road. Drivers must yield to trains at these crossings.

Question 335: What is a "School Zone" sign?

Answer: A sign indicating a zone near a school where speed limits are reduced during certain times.

Explanation: A "School Zone" sign is used to alert drivers that they are entering a zone near a school where children may be present, and where speed limits are often reduced during school hours for safety.

Question 336: What is a "Speed Limit" sign?

Answer: A sign indicating the maximum legal speed for a section of road.

Explanation: A "Speed Limit" sign is used to inform drivers of the maximum legal speed they are allowed to drive on a certain section of road. Drivers must not exceed this speed under normal driving conditions.

Question 337: What is a "No Parking" sign?

Answer: A sign indicating that parking is not allowed in a certain area.

Explanation: A "No Parking" sign is used to designate areas where it is illegal to park a vehicle, either at all times or during certain hours.

Question 338: What is a "No U-turn" sign?

Answer: A sign indicating that U-turns are not permitted.

Explanation: A "No U-turn" sign is used to indicate locations where it is illegal to make a U-turn, or a 180-degree turn to reverse the direction of travel.

Question 339: What is a "Left Turn Yield on Green" sign?

Answer: A sign indicating that left-turning traffic must yield to oncoming traffic when the signal is green.

Explanation: A "Left Turn Yield on Green" sign is used at intersections where left-turning traffic does not have a dedicated left-turn signal and must yield to oncoming traffic when the signal is green.

Question 341: What is a "Rest Area" sign?

Answer: A sign indicating a roadside area where drivers can rest, use restroom facilities, and sometimes get food and fuel.

Explanation: A "Rest Area" sign is used to alert drivers to upcoming locations where they can take a break from driving. These areas often have parking, restroom facilities, picnic areas, and sometimes vending machines or other services.

Question 342: What is a "Hospital" sign?
Answer: A sign indicating the direction to a nearby hospital.
Explanation: A "Hospital" sign is used to direct drivers to the nearest hospital. It is generally marked with a blue 'H' symbol.
Question 343: What is a "Bike Lane" sign?
Answer: A sign indicating a lane designated for bicycle use.
Explanation: A "Bike Lane" sign is used to mark lanes that are reserved for bicycles. These lanes are typically delineated with painted lines and bicycle symbols on the road surface.
Question 344: What is a "Merge" sign?
Answer: A sign indicating that two lanes of traffic are coming together into one lane.
Explanation: A "Merge" sign is used to alert drivers that they will need to merge with other traffic, typically because one lane is ending.
Question 345: What is a "Lane Ends" sign?
Answer: A sign indicating that a lane on the road is about to end.
Explanation: A "Lane Ends" sign is used to warn drivers that their lane is about to end and they will need to merge with traffic in another lane.
Question 346: What is a "School Bus Stop Ahead" sign?
Answer: A sign indicating that a school bus stop is ahead on the road.
Explanation: A "School Bus Stop Ahead" sign is used to warn drivers that they are approaching a location where a school bus may stop to pick up or drop off children.
Question 347: What is a "Slippery When Wet" sign?
Answer: A sign indicating that a section of road may be slippery when wet or raining.
Explanation: A "Slippery When Wet" sign is used to alert drivers to potential hazardous conditions when it's raining or the road is wet.
Question 348: What is a "Divided Highway Begins" sign?
Answer: A sign indicating that the road will soon split into separate lanes for each direction, typically divided by a median.
Explanation: A "Divided Highway Begins" sign is used to inform drivers that they are approaching a section of road where the lanes for each direction of traffic are separated by a median or barrier.
Question 349: What is a "Divided Highway Ends" sign?
Answer: A sign indicating that the divided highway is about to end, and the road will soon have two-way traffic without a median separating the directions.
Explanation: A "Divided Highway Ends" sign is used to inform

drivers that they are leaving a divided highway and approaching a section of road with two-way traffic.
Question 350: What is a "No Passing Zone" sign?
Answer: A sign indicating that it is not safe to pass other vehicles due to conditions such as limited visibility or oncoming traffic.
Explanation: A "No Passing Zone" sign is used to warn drivers that due to road conditions, they should not attempt to pass other vehicles in that area.
Question 351: What is a "Pass With Care" sign?
Answer: A sign indicating that passing is allowed, but drivers should do so with caution.
Explanation: A "Pass With Care" sign is used to inform drivers that they may pass slower vehicles on the road, but they should do so cautiously and only when it's safe.
Question 352: What is a "Truck Route" sign?
Answer: A sign indicating a route designed for truck travel.
Explanation: A "Truck Route" sign is used to direct truck drivers to routes that are suitable for large or heavy vehicles, often avoiding areas with low bridges, narrow roads, or residential areas.
Question 353: What is a "No Outlet" sign?
Answer: A sign indicating that a road does not have any exit or connection to another road.
Explanation: A "No Outlet" sign is used to alert drivers that a street or road does not lead anywhere else or have any exit, often used in cul-de-sacs or dead ends.
Question 354: What is a "Keep Right" sign?
Answer: A sign indicating that drivers should stay to the right of a traffic island, median, or obstacle.
Explanation: A "Keep Right" sign is often used where the road is divided or there's an obstruction on the road. It instructs drivers to pass to the right of the sign or obstacle, and not to the left.
Question 355: What is a "Yield" sign?
Answer: A sign that instructs drivers to slow down and give way to traffic in the intersection they are crossing or road they are entering.
Explanation: A "Yield" sign is a triangular sign, typically red and white, which means that a driver must prepare to stop if necessary to let other drivers on the road continue.
Question 356: What is a "No U-Turn" sign?
Answer: A sign that prohibits drivers from making a U-turn.
Explanation: A "No U-Turn" sign is used to inform drivers that U-turns are illegal in that area, often due to safety reasons.

Question 357: What is a "Stop" sign?
Answer: A sign that instructs drivers to come to a complete stop, and not proceed until it is safe to do so.
Explanation: A "Stop" sign is an octagonal sign, usually red with white letters, that requires drivers to stop fully before proceeding.
Question 358: What is a "Do Not Enter" sign?
Answer: A sign indicating that a road or area is off limits to certain traffic, often used at the exit of one-way roads.
Explanation: A "Do Not Enter" sign is used to prevent vehicles from entering a certain area or road, such as the wrong direction of a one-way street.
Question 359: What is a "Speed Limit" sign?
Answer: A sign indicating the maximum legal speed for a section of road.
Explanation: A "Speed Limit" sign is used to inform drivers of the maximum legal speed they are allowed to drive on that section of road.
Question 360: What is a "One Way" sign?
Answer: A sign indicating that a street or roadway allows traffic to flow in one direction only.
Explanation: A "One Way" sign is used on one-way streets and intersections to keep traffic flowing smoothly in one direction.
Question 361: What is a "Road Work Ahead" sign?
Answer: A sign indicating upcoming road construction or maintenance activities.
Explanation: A "Road Work Ahead" sign is used to warn drivers of construction or maintenance activities on the road ahead, so they can slow down and prepare for any road conditions or detours.
Question 362: What is a "Detour" sign?
Answer: A sign indicating an alternate route for drivers to take, usually due to road work or a closed road.
Explanation: A "Detour" sign is used to guide drivers around road work, a closed road, or other obstruction.
Question 363: What is a "Roundabout" sign?
Answer: A sign indicating that drivers are approaching a roundabout intersection.
Explanation: A "Roundabout" sign is used to warn drivers that they are approaching a circular intersection where traffic flows continuously in one direction around a central island.
Question 364: What is a "Pedestrian Crossing" sign?
Answer: A sign indicating a designated area where pedestrians may cross the road.
Explanation: A "Pedestrian Crossing" sign is used to alert drivers

to areas where pedestrians may be crossing the road, and to remind drivers to yield to people crossing.
Question 365: What is a "Railroad Crossing" sign?
Answer: A sign indicating that a railroad track crosses the road.
Explanation: A "Railroad Crossing" sign is used to warn drivers that they are approaching a location where a railroad track crosses the road at grade.
Question 366: What is a "School Zone" sign?
Answer: A sign indicating a zone near a school where speed limits are reduced during certain hours.
Explanation: A "School Zone" sign is used to alert drivers to areas near schools where speed limits are reduced during school hours to protect children.
Question 367: What is a "Deer Crossing" sign?
Answer: A sign indicating an area where deer frequently cross the road.
Explanation: A "Deer Crossing" sign is used to warn drivers of areas where deer or other large animals may be crossing the road, especially in rural or wooded areas.
Question 368: What is a "Handicap Parking" sign?
Answer: A sign indicating a parking space reserved for vehicles displaying a handicap placard or license plate.
Explanation: A "Handicap Parking" sign is used to designate parking spaces that are reserved for use by specific individuals .

Question 369: What is a "Slow Moving Vehicle" sign?
Answer: A sign used on vehicles that move slowly (25 mph or less) on public roads to alert other drivers to this fact.
Explanation: A "Slow Moving Vehicle" sign is typically a reflective orange triangle bordered in red, used to warn other motorists that the vehicle displaying the sign is moving slower than the normal speed of traffic.
Question 370: What is a "Men at Work" sign?
Answer: A sign indicating that there are workers on or near the roadway, typically in a construction zone.
Explanation: A "Men at Work" sign is used to alert drivers to construction zones where workers may be present, so they can slow down and drive with extra caution.
Question 371: What is a "Bump" sign?
Answer: A sign indicating that there is a bump or uneven surface on the road ahead.
Explanation: A "Bump" sign is used to warn drivers to slow down for a sudden change in road elevation or a rough patch of road.

Question 372: What is a "Weight Limit" sign?
Answer: A sign indicating the maximum weight a vehicle can be to use a certain road or bridge.
Explanation: A "Weight Limit" sign is used to protect roads and bridges from potential damage caused by heavy vehicles. Vehicles exceeding the weight limit indicated on the sign are prohibited from using that road or bridge.
Question 373: What is a "Traffic Signal Ahead" sign?
Answer: A sign indicating that there is a traffic light ahead.
Explanation: A "Traffic Signal Ahead" sign is used to warn drivers of an upcoming intersection controlled by traffic lights, particularly when the lights are not visible from a distance.
Question 374: What is a "Falling Rocks" sign?
Answer: A sign warning of potential falling rocks or debris from adjacent cliffs or hillsides.
Explanation: A "Falling Rocks" sign is used in areas where there is a risk of rocks or other debris falling onto the road, such as near cliffs or steep hills.
Question 375: What is a "Steep Hill Downward" sign?
Answer: A sign warning drivers that they are approaching a steep downhill grade.
Explanation: A "Steep Hill Downward" sign is used to warn drivers that the road is about to descend at a steep grade, which can affect vehicle control, especially for heavy vehicles or those towing trailers.
Question 376: What is a "Steep Hill Upward" sign?
Answer: A sign warning drivers that they are approaching a steep uphill grade.
Explanation: A "Steep Hill Upward" sign is used to warn drivers that the road is about to ascend at a steep grade, which may require downshifting or increased engine power to maintain speed.
Question 377: What is a "Sharp Turn" sign?
Answer: A sign warning drivers of an upcoming sharp turn in the road.
Explanation: A "Sharp Turn" sign is used to warn drivers of a sudden, sharp turn in the road ahead, so they can slow down and prepare to navigate the turn safely.
Question 378: What is a "Narrow Bridge" sign?
Answer: A sign warning drivers that they are approaching a bridge with narrow lanes.
Explanation: A "Narrow Bridge" sign is used to warn drivers that the bridge ahead is not as wide as the approaching road, and they should be prepared to adjust their speed and position accordingly.

Question 379: What is a "Y Intersection" sign?
Answer: A sign warning of an upcoming intersection where a road splits into two different directions.
Explanation: A "Y Intersection" sign is used to warn drivers that they will soon reach a point where the road splits into two separate roads at a Y-shaped intersection.
Question 380: What is a "Double Curve" sign?
Answer: A sign warning drivers of two successive curves in the road ahead.
Explanation: A "Double Curve" sign is used to warn drivers of two successive curves in the road, with the first curve bending in the direction shown on the sign.
Question 381: What is a "Cross Road" sign?
Answer: A sign warning drivers of an upcoming intersection with another road that crosses their path at a 90-degree angle.
Explanation: A "Cross Road" sign is used to warn drivers of an upcoming intersection with a road that intersects their path from the left and right.
Question 382: What is a "Pedestrians Only" sign?
Answer: A sign indicating a zone or path where only pedestriansare allowed.
Explanation: A "Pedestrians Only" sign is used to designate certain paths or areas where only foot traffic is permitted, and vehicles are not allowed.
Question 383: What is a "No Bicycles" sign?
Answer: A sign indicating that bicycles are not permitted on a certain road, path, or area.
Explanation: A "No Bicycles" sign is used to designate areas where bicycling is not allowed, for reasons of safety, traffic flow, or other regulations.
Question 384: What is a "No U-Turn" sign?
Answer: A sign indicating that U-turns are not permitted at a certain location.
Explanation: A "No U-Turn" sign is used to forbid drivers from making a U-turn, typically because it would be unsafe or disrupt the flow of traffic.
Question 385: What is a "No Right Turn" sign?
Answer: A sign indicating that right turns are not permitted at a certain intersection or location.
Explanation: A "No Right Turn" sign is used to forbid drivers from turning right, typically because it would be unsafe or disrupt the flow of traffic.

Question 386: What is a "No Left Turn" sign?
Answer: A sign indicating that left turns are not permitted at a certain intersection or location.
Explanation: A "No Left Turn" sign is used to forbid drivers from turning left, typically because it would be unsafe or disrupt the flow of traffic.
Question 387: What is a "No Entry" sign?
Answer: A sign indicating that entry is not permitted into a certain area or road.
Explanation: A "No Entry" sign is used to designate areas or roads where entry is not allowed, typically to control the direction of traffic or prevent access to restricted areas.
Question 388: What is a "No Parking" sign?
Answer: A sign indicating that parking is not allowed in a certain area.
Explanation: A "No Parking" sign is used to designate areas where vehicles are not permitted to park, either at all times or during certain hours.
Question 389: What is a "School Zone" sign?
Answer: A sign indicating a zone near a school where traffic laws are strictly enforced and speed limits are often reduced during school hours.
Explanation: A "School Zone" sign is used to alert drivers that they are entering an area near a school where children may be present, and where they need to be particularly cautious and abide by any posted speed reductions or other traffic laws.
Question 390: What is a "Hospital Zone" sign?
Answer: A sign indicating a zone near a hospital where traffic laws are strictly enforced and drivers should be particularly cautious.
Explanation: A "Hospital Zone" sign is used to alert drivers that they are entering an area near a hospital, where they should drive cautiously, be prepared for ambulances, and abide by any posted traffic laws.
Question 391: What is a "Fire Station Zone" sign?
Answer: A sign indicating a zone near a fire station where traffic laws are strictly enforced and drivers should be particularly cautious.
Explanation: A "Fire Station Zone" sign is used to alert drivers that they are entering an area near a fire station, where they should drive cautiously, be prepared for fire trucks, and abide by any posted traffic laws.
Question 392: What is a "Deer Crossing" sign?
Answer: A sign warning drivers of an area where deer or other

large animals are known to cross the road.
Explanation: A "Deer Crossing" sign is used in areas where deer or other large animals are often seen crossing the road, to alert drivers to the potential hazard and encourage them to drive cautiously.
Question 393: What is a "Truck Route" sign?
Answer: A sign indicating a route specifically designed for trucks or heavy vehicles.
Explanation: A "Truck Route" sign is used to designate certain roads or routes that are suitable for trucks or heavy vehicles, taking into account factors like road width, bridge height and weight limits, and traffic flow.
Question 394: What is a "Bicycle Route" sign?
Answer: A sign indicating a route specifically designed for bicycles.
Explanation: A "Bicycle Route" sign is used to designate certain roads or paths that are suitable for bicycle traffic, often as part of a larger network of bicycle-friendly routes.
Question 395: What is a "Pedestrian Crossing" sign?
Answer: A sign warning drivers of a designated pedestrian crossing.
Explanation: A "Pedestrian Crossing" sign is used to alert drivers to areas where pedestrians may be crossing the road
Question 396: What is a "Shared Use Paths" sign?
Answer: A sign indicating a path that is shared by pedestrians, cyclists, and sometimes other users.
Explanation: A "Shared Use Paths" sign is used to designate paths that are designed for use by both pedestrians and cyclists, and possibly other users like rollerbladers or skateboarders.
Question 397: What is a "Stop Ahead" sign?
Answer: A sign warning drivers that there is a stop sign ahead.
Explanation: A "Stop Ahead" sign is used to alert drivers that a stop sign is coming up, particularly in cases where the stop sign may not be immediately visible due to a curve, hill, or other obstruction.
Question 398: What is a "Yield Ahead" sign?
Answer: A sign warning drivers that there is a yield sign ahead.
Explanation: A "Yield Ahead" sign is used to alert drivers that a yield sign is coming up, particularly in cases where the yield sign may not be immediately visible due to a curve, hill, or other obstruction.
Question 399: What is a "Railroad Crossing Ahead" sign?
Answer: A sign warning drivers that there is a railroad crossing ahead.

Explanation: A "Railroad Crossing Ahead" sign is used to alert drivers to the presence of a railroad crossing ahead, so they can prepare to stop if a train is coming.
Question 400: What is a "Merge Left/Right" sign?
Answer: A sign warning drivers that they will need to merge into the left or right lane ahead.
Explanation: A "Merge Left/Right" sign is used to alert drivers that they will need to merge due to a lane ending or other changes in the road layout.
Question 401: What is a "Lane Ends" sign?
Answer: A sign warning drivers that their lane is ending and they will need to merge into another lane.
Explanation: A "Lane Ends" sign is used to alert drivers that their current lane is coming to an end, and they will need to merge safely into the adjacent lane.
Question 402: What is a "Speed Limit" sign?
Answer: A sign indicating the maximum legal speed that vehicles can travel on a particular road.
Explanation: A "Speed Limit" sign is used to inform drivers of the maximum legal speed for the road they are on, which they must not exceed.
Question 403: What is a "One Way" sign?
Answer: A sign indicating that traffic flows in one direction only.
Explanation: A "One Way" sign is used on roads where traffic is only allowed to flow in the direction indicated by the sign.
Question 404: What is a "Two Way Traffic" sign?
Answer: A sign indicating that traffic flows in both directions.
Explanation: A "Two Way Traffic" sign is used on roads where traffic is allowed to flow in both directions, typically with each direction having its own lane or lanes.
Question 405: What is a "Divided Highway Begins" sign?
Answer: A sign warning drivers that they are approaching a section of road that is divided into separate lanes for each direction by a median or physical barrier.
Explanation: A "Divided Highway Begins" sign is used to warn drivers that they are about to enter a section of road where the lanes for each direction of travel are separated by a median or physical barrier.
Question 406: What is a "Divided Highway Ends" sign?
Answer: A sign warning drivers that the divided section of the road is ending, and the road will no longer have separate lanes for each direction.
Explanation: A "Divided Highway Ends" sign is used to warn

drivers that the divided section of the road is coming to an end, and the lanes for each direction of travel will no longer be separated by a median or physical barrier.

Question 407: What is a "No Passing Zone" sign?
Answer: A sign indicating a stretch of road where passing other vehicles is prohibited.
Explanation: A "No Passing Zone" sign is used to designate stretches of road where it is unsafe or illegal to pass other vehicles, typically due to limited visibility, narrow lanes, or other safety considerations.

Question 408: What is a "Pass With Care" sign?
Answer: A sign indicating a stretch of road where passing other vehicles is allowed, but drivers should do so with caution.
Explanation: A "Pass With Care" sign is used to designate stretches of road where passing is allowed, but drivers should exercise caution due to potential oncoming traffic, narrow road widths, or other factors.

Question 409: What is a "Slippery When Wet" sign?
Answer: A sign warning drivers that the road may be slippery and hazardous when it's wet or raining.
Explanation: A "Slippery When Wet" sign is used to warn drivers that the road surface may become slippery in wet conditions, which can increase the risk of skidding and accidents.

Question 410: What is a "Right Lane Must Turn Right" sign?
Answer: A sign indicating that vehicles in the right lane must make a right turn at the intersection.
Explanation: A "Right Lane Must Turn Right" sign is used to indicate to drivers that if they are in the right lane, they must make a right turn at the intersection ahead.

Question 411: What is a "Left Lane Must Turn Left" sign?
Answer: A sign indicating that vehicles in the left lane must make a left turn at the intersection.
Explanation: A "Left Lane Must Turn Left" sign is used to indicate to drivers that if they are in the left lane, they must make a left turn at the intersection ahead.

Question 412: What is a "Center Lane Left Turn Only" sign?
Answer: A sign indicating that the center lane is reserved for vehicles making left turns only.
Explanation: A "Center Lane Left Turn Only" sign is used to designate a center lane where vehicles can only make a left turn. This helps manage traffic flow and reduce confusion at intersections.

Question 413: What is a "School Zone" sign?
Answer: A sign warning drivers that they are approaching a school zone, where speed limits are often reduced during school hours and drivers are expected to be extra cautious.
Explanation: A "School Zone" sign is used to signal to drivers that they are entering an area where children may be present, especially during school hours. Drivers are required to reduce speed and exercise increased caution.
Question 414: What is a "Pedestrian Crossing" sign?
Answer: A sign warning drivers to watch for pedestrians crossing the road.
Explanation: A "Pedestrian Crossing" sign is used to indicate a designated point on the road where pedestrians may cross. Drivers are expected to yield to pedestrians at these points.
Question 415: What is a "Bike Lane" sign?
Answer: A sign indicating a lane designated for bicycle traffic.
Explanation: A "Bike Lane" sign is used to designate a lane for bicycles. These lanes are typically marked with bike symbols and/or signs, and are for the exclusive use of cyclists.
Question 416: What is a "No U-Turn" sign?
Answer: A sign prohibiting drivers from making a U-turn.
Explanation: A "No U-Turn" sign is used to inform drivers that making a U-turn at the location is illegal. These signs are typically installed at intersections or points on the road where U-turns could be dangerous or disrupt traffic flow.
Question 417: What is a "No Right Turn" sign?
Answer: A sign prohibiting drivers from making a right turn.
Explanation: A "No Right Turn" sign is used to inform drivers that making a right turn at the location is illegal. This could be due to specific traffic patterns, construction, road layout, or safety concerns.
Question 418: What is a "No Left Turn" sign?
Answer: A sign prohibiting drivers from making a left turn.
Explanation: A "No Left Turn" sign is used to inform drivers that making a left turn at the location is illegal. This could be due to specific traffic patterns, construction, road layout, or safety concerns.
Question 419: What is a "No Trucks" sign?
Answer: A sign prohibiting trucks from entering a certain road or area.
Explanation: A "No Trucks" sign is used to inform truck drivers that they are not allowed to use a certain road or area. This could

be because the road is not designed to handle heavy vehicles, or due to local regulations or noise restrictions.
Question 420: What is a "Truck Route" sign?
Answer: A sign indicating a route designated for trucks.
Explanation: A "Truck Route" sign is used to guide truck drivers to routes that are suitable for heavy vehicles. These routes are typically designed to handle the weight and size of trucks and may avoid residential areas or roads with low bridges or tight turns.
Question 421: What is a "No Parking" sign?
Answer: A sign indicating a zone where parking is not allowed.
Explanation: A "No Parking" sign is used to denote areas where vehicles are not allowed to park.
Question 422: What is an "Emergency Parking Only" sign?
Answer: A sign indicating a zone where parking is permitted only in case of an emergency.
Explanation: An "Emergency Parking Only" sign is used to designate areas where vehicles can only stop or park in case of an emergency. This helps to keep these areas clear for emergency vehicles or situations.
Question 423: What is a "No Pedestrian Crossing" sign?
Answer: A sign indicating that pedestrians are not permitted to cross the road at that point.
Explanation: A "No Pedestrian Crossing" sign is used to inform pedestrians that they are not allowed to cross the road at that location. This is often due to safety reasons, such as high-speed traffic or poor visibility.
Question 424: What is a "No Bicycles" sign?
Answer: A sign indicating that bicycles are not allowed on that particular road or area.
Explanation: A "No Bicycles" sign is used to inform cyclists that they are not allowed to use a certain road or area. This is often due to safety considerations, such as high-speed traffic or poor visibility.
Question 425: What is a "No Right on Red" sign?
Answer: A sign indicating that drivers are not permitted to make a right turn at a red light.
Explanation: A "No Right on Red" sign is used at certain intersections to inform drivers that they are not allowed to make a right turn while the traffic signal is red. The purpose is often to protect pedestrians who may be crossing at the same time.
Question 426: What is a "No Left on Red" sign?
Answer: A sign indicating that drivers are not permitted to make a left turn at a red light.

Explanation: A "No Left on Red" sign is used at certain intersections to inform drivers that they are not allowed to make a left turn while the traffic signal is red. Like the "No Right on Red" sign, the purpose is often to protect pedestrians who may be crossing at the same time.
Question 427: What is a "No Turn on Red" sign?
Answer: A sign indicating that drivers are not permitted to make any turns at a red light.
Explanation: A "No Turn on Red" sign is used at certain intersections to inform drivers that they are not allowed to make any turns (left or right) while the traffic signal is red. This is usually done to protect pedestrians and to manage traffic flow.
Question 428: What is a "Keep Right" sign?
Answer: A sign indicating that drivers should keep to the right of a traffic island, median, or obstruction.
Explanation: A "Keep Right" sign is used to guide drivers to stay to the right of a traffic island, median, or obstruction. It helps manage traffic flow and prevent head-on collisions.
Question 429: What is a "Keep Left" sign?
Answer: A sign indicating that drivers should keep to the left of a traffic island, median, or obstruction.
Explanation: A "Keep Left" sign is used to guide drivers to stay to the left of a traffic island, median, or obstruction. Like the "Keep Right" sign, it helps manage traffic flow and prevent head-on collisions.
Question 430: What is a "Do Not Enter" sign?
Answer: A sign indicating that vehicles are not allowed to enter the road or area.
Explanation: A "Do Not Enter" sign is used to indicate a road or area where vehicles are not allowed to enter, usually because it is a one-way street or a restricted area.
Question 431: What is a "Wrong Way" sign?
Answer: A sign indicating that a vehicle is moving in the wrong direction on a roadway.
Explanation: A "Wrong Way" sign is used to alert drivers who have entered a roadway in the wrong direction. These signs are typically placed on freeway off-ramps or one-way streets to prevent head-on collisions.
Question 432: What is a "No Outlet" sign?
Answer: A sign indicating that a street does not have any exit or is a dead-end street.
Explanation: A "No Outlet" sign is used to denote a street or road that does not have another exit, often referred to as a cul-de-sac

or dead-end. This can help drivers avoid getting lost or entering residential areas unnecessarily.
Question 433: What is a "No Thru Traffic" sign?
Answer: A sign indicating a road or area that cannot be used as a through route.
Explanation: A "No Thru Traffic" sign is used to inform drivers that aparticular road or area should not be used as a shortcut or bypass to other streets. The purpose is to minimize unnecessary traffic, especially in residential areas or school zones.
Question 434: What is a "No U-Turn" sign?
Answer: A sign indicating that U-turns are not permitted.
Explanation: A "No U-Turn" sign is used to inform drivers that they are not permitted to make a U-turn at a specific location. This is typically due to safety considerations, such as limited visibility or high-speed traffic.
Question 435: What is a "No Trucks" sign?
Answer: A sign indicating that trucks or other large vehicles are not permitted on a specific road.
Explanation: A "No Trucks" sign is used to inform drivers of large vehicles that they are not permitted to use a specific road or area. This is often due to the road's physical constraints (e.g., low bridges, narrow lanes) or to minimize noise and pollution in residential areas.
Question 436: What is a "Yield" sign?
Answer: A sign requiring drivers to give way to traffic on the road they are crossing or entering.
Explanation: A "Yield" sign is used to indicate that drivers must slow down or stop if necessary to allow other vehicles or pedestrians to proceed first. It is typically used where roads merge or intersect and it is not necessary to stop traffic flow entirely.
Question 437: What is a "Stop" sign?
Answer: A sign requiring drivers to come to a complete stop before proceeding.
Explanation: A "Stop" sign is used to indicate that drivers must come to a complete stop before proceeding. It is typically used at intersections to prevent collisions by ensuring that only one vehicle moves into the intersection at a time.
Question 438: What is a "Speed Limit" sign?
Answer: A sign indicating the maximum legal speed for vehicles traveling on a particular road.
Explanation: A "Speed Limit" sign is used to inform drivers of the maximum speed at which they are legally allowed to travel on a particular road. The limit is set based on various factors, including

the type of road, its physical condition, and the surrounding environment.
Question 439: What is a "School Zone" sign?
Answer: A sign indicating a zone near a school where special traffic rules apply.
Explanation: A "School Zone" sign is used to mark areas near schools where traffic speeds are reduced during certain times of the day to ensure the safety of students. Drivers are required to slow down and be extra vigilant for children in these zones.
Question 440: What is a "Pedestrian Crossing" sign?
Answer: A sign indicating a designated point where pedestrians may cross the road.
Explanation: A "Pedestrian Crossing" sign is used to mark designated points on the road where pedestrians are expected to cross. Drivers are required to yield to pedestrians at these crossings.
Question 441: What is a "One Way" sign?
Answer: A sign indicating that traffic is allowed to move in only one direction on a specific road.
Explanation: A "One Way" sign is used to indicate that traffic on a particular road is allowed to move in only one direction. This helps to manage traffic flow and prevent head-on collisions.
Question 442: What is a "Merging Traffic" sign?
Answer: A sign warning drivers that two separate roadways will be converging into one.
Explanation: A "Merging Traffic" sign is used to alert drivers that they will need to either allow another vehicle to merge into their lane from another roadway or that they themselves will need to merge into another lane.
Question 443: What is a "Lane Ends" sign?
Answer: A sign warning drivers that their lane is ending soon and they will need to merge into another lane.
Explanation: A "Lane Ends" sign is used to alert drivers that their current lane will soon end, requiring them to merge into another lane. It helps to manage traffic flow and prevent sudden lane changes.
Question 444: What is a "Hospital" sign?
Answer: A sign indicating the location of a hospital or the direction to a nearby hospital.
Explanation: A "Hospital" sign is used to guide drivers to the location of a hospital. It could indicate that a hospital is on the next turn, at a certain distance, or just directly ahead.

Question 445: What is a "Fire Station" sign?
Answer: A sign indicating the location of a fire station or the direction to a nearby fire station.
Explanation: A "Fire Station" sign is used to guide drivers to the location of a fire station. It can also serve as a warning for drivers to be cautious of fire engines entering or exiting the station.
Question 446: What is a "Road Work Ahead" sign?
Answer: A sign warning drivers of construction or maintenance activities on the road ahead.
Explanation: A "Road Work Ahead" sign is used to alert drivers that there are ongoing construction or maintenance activities on the road ahead. This sign helps ensure the safety of the workers and the drivers by encouraging drivers to slow down and be cautious.
Question 447: What is a "Detour" sign?
Answer: A sign indicating a temporary route for traffic to follow due to a road closure.
Explanation: A "Detour" sign is used to guide drivers along a temporary route when the usual route is closed for some reason, such as construction, an accident, or a special event.
Question 448: What is a "Roundabout" sign?
Answer: A sign indicating that a roundabout intersection is ahead.
Explanation: A "Roundabout" sign is used to alert drivers that they are approaching a roundabout intersection, where traffic flows in one direction around a central island.
Question 449: What is a "Slippery When Wet" sign?
Answer: A sign warning drivers that the road surface may become slippery under wet conditions.
Explanation: A "Slippery When Wet" sign is used to warn drivers that the road surface may become slippery and potentially hazardous under wet conditions, such as during rain or when there is ice or snow.
Question 450: What is a "Falling Rocks" sign?
Answer: A sign warning drivers of potential falling rocks from adjacent cliffs or mountains.
Explanation: A "Falling Rocks" sign is used to alert drivers that they are in an area where rocks or other debris might fall onto the roadway, typically in mountainous or hilly areas.

Made in the USA
Las Vegas, NV
15 October 2023

79175275R00059